Marketing to Generation X

Marketing to Generation X

Karen Ritchie

LEXINGTON BOOKS
An Imprint of The Free Press
NEW YORK   LONDON   TORONTO   SYDNEY   TOKYO   SINGAPORE

THE FREE PRESS
A Division of Simon & Schuster
1230 Avenue of the Americas
New York, NY 10020

THE FREE PRESS and colophon are trademarks
of Simon & Schuster Inc.

Manufactured in the United States of America

10 9 8 7 6 5 4 3 2 1

Library of Congress Cataloging-In-Publication Data
        Ritchie, Karen.
Marketing to Generation X / Karen Ritchie.
p. cm.
        Includes bibliographical references and index.
        ISBN: 0-7432-3658-0
1. Marketing   2. Youth as consumers.   I. Title
HF5415.R5524   1995
658.8'348—dc20
CIP

For information regarding special discounts for bulk purchases, please contact Simon &
Schuster Special Sales at 1-800-456-6798 or business@simonandschuster.com

This book is dedicated to Kirsten and Kendra,
who made me care about Generation X,
and to Dan,
who learned to cook

Contents

Foreword by Bob Guccione, Jr.   *vii*

1. How I Got Started   1

2. Why Bother?   11

3. What Did We Do to Deserve Them?   27

4. Diversity Reigns!   51

5. Mass Media: The Wonder Years   63

6. Growing Up X: Rumor, Scandal, and Trash TV   85

7. Interactivity and the New Media   113

8. Consumer Behavior: Choosing Brand X   129

9. Future X: Implications for Marketing.   151

10. The Future of Advertising   163

References   *169*
Index   *173*
Acknowledgments   *177*

Foreword

Oscar Wilde predicted and dismissed Generation X over a hundred years ago when he said "Youth is wasted on the young." He foresaw the slackers, the nonchalance bordering on indolence, the oddly contradictory mix of foolish romanticism and even more foolish cynicism. In one phrase he summed up the inability of young people to express (coherently at least) and define themselves, to concentrate and be seriously responsible, and even to capitalize on the precious vitality and opportunity that appears, with hindsight, to be the effortless and infinite currency of youth. And, of course, he was wrong.

We all know what he meant, and those of us past youth may feel the tug of his impossible fantasy, to know when we were younger what age has taught us, but Wilde's quip is equivalent to saying that life is wasted on the dying. Life is the *process* of dying—every exhaled breath is a footstep closer to expiration. Few people—and no sane ones—see that as a reason to abandon life, to hasten death. We just accept it, shrug our shoulders, and do as much as we can to lengthen the process.

And youth itself is a process, a life within one's total life. But the prosecutors of so-called Generation X, having already convicted them in absentia of that awful name, have successfully prevented the plea of "process" from being admitted into the debate. The rest of humanity—particularly us older people—are allowed to live to the rhythms of our age, with no unreasonable expectations. But, suddenly, in the past few years, young people between eighteen and thirty-four have been hauled before some Kafka-esque court and charged with the illogical crime of not being completely adults, and therefore failures. When young people complain, rightly, that they have been sucker punched, this is turned against them, as proof that they are nothing more than piteous whiners. In the kangaroo court of America's generally socially deteriorated culture, young people have been convicted of being young and await their sentencing.

The wrong generation is on trial, but that was deliberate and the real culprits, the people who mortgaged the future and absconded with the money, have long escaped by now and if we could even summon the energy to pursue them, we probably wouldn't have the resolve to prosecute and punish them, because it would require effort and self-reflection, two things our society lost its courage for some time ago. The villains know this and in fact, literally, banked on it.

I don't think any one person conceived of the brilliant scheme to blame the next generation, to accuse the heirs of blowing the as-yet-uninherited inheritance. It was all part of a mass consciousness, each individual's contribution imperceptible, virtually molecular. In fact, the author of this book, in her shrewd insight that the approaching generation was already here, not safely off in the eveningless distance, may have unwittingly been the impetus for the surge against youth, the air of her intelligent observations and conclusions gathered and reshaped into the wind of the first shout of "J'accuse," which quickly led to a mob lynching of a definitively blameless generation.

Karen has a superb sense of human nature. She saw the next generation taking its formidable shape as a silhouette against the relief of Boomers dismissing young people as losers. She knew that only when a community senses their receding potency do they attack people whose potency is increasing. She strode to a podium at a magazine publisher's conference (she'll tell you this better herself) and gave the speech that was heard (at least repeated) around the world: the Baby Boomers era was effectively over; the day belonged to the young.

I know Karen did not intentionally set off the firestorm that followed. She'd intended to change a thirty-year ingrained cultural paradigm, that the sun would never set on the Boomers, presumed, by themselves, to be God's own favorite sons and daughters. She didn't intend to crucify anyone, least of all the people who were our cruel God's new favorite sons and daughters. But no sooner had her pronouncement landed on the front page of U.S. newspapers' business sections, than magazine and newspaper "lifestyle" editors were simultaneously discovering and burying alive 65 million young adults. The epithet "Generation X" stuck like unshakable toilet tissue to the shoe of every young person in America, the great majority of whom were trotted out for every local and national TV news show, positioned under the tungsten lights, and gawked at, prodded and generally encouraged to communicate ("Are you a friendly people? Do you come on a mission of peace, or to enslave us?"). In media coast to coast, young people *were* treated like aliens, as if they had suddenly dropped out of the sky, ironically and quixotically, often by people their own age.

Along with the insulting moniker—their "X" this century's scarlet letter—went the awful image, hardening fast on them like lacquer. They were shiftless, indifferent, and, if their attention span lasted long enough for them to start something they could give up on, quitters. They only watched mindless TV or MTV, which was separated out as a kind of refined degree of mindlessness, listened to nihilistic and unharmonious rock and rap music, disavowed solid American values and conventions (like marriage, religion, and, you know, employment). They read magazines like *SPIN*— poor, lost souls. Oh, and of course they killed themselves pretty regularly and for sex they had AIDS, which, once you got to thinking about it, was probably their fault.

This first explosion of hysteria happened at the end of 1992, when such youth culture-sensitive publications as *Atlantic Monthly* and *The New Republic* had the duelling cover stories about who and what Generation X was. You'd have thought they were explaining a new virus and the people most commonly afflicted with it as they dourly, and with a heavy air of sageliness, gave their eulogies for the first generation that was not going to be able to do as well as its parents. Their bottom line was that Generation X was stillborn—that the monster had died in its horrible childbirth.

In January 1993, I wrote an Op-Ed for the *L.A. Times,* and reprinted it in *SPIN,* saying that the personification of Generation X was a deliberate propaganda campaign intended to make young people seem less desirable to employers, thus preserving jobs and career options for the Boomers, and slowing the next generation's succession to power.

I implored young readers not to be distracted by the attempt to categorize them, and not to fall into the easy and understandable trap of becoming cynical, that this was precisely what their elders wanted them to do. I also said that I believed Boomers—my generation—were guilty of raping the economy and the environment and that young people were inheriting a bankrupted American Dream but in that adversity was an opportunity to remake American society and rebuild American ideals, and that they, the new generation, could and probably would make a new and better world.

The sociological conditions facing this generation are the most important aspect of the equation of how they will fare, yet, other than dire predictions about the job market, it's never discussed. Neither is the fact that all of our fates are inextricably intertwined: it's not as if the future is the sole province of people under thirty—everything influences everybody.

This ignoring of the real issue is what makes the debate about Generation X as hollow as its title. The focus is always on whether or not people now eighteen to thirty-four will amount to much in the future—a deliberately meaningless point, since it's as valid as critiquing a painting before the artist has finished painting it. It's designed to inflame the young person into righteous denials of their alleged worthlessness: an abstract response to an abstract proposition. But an energy consuming one, therefore strategically valuable to the older generation trying to keep the new one at bay. The debate is also hollow because no one, on either side, is disputing that the rising generation is a huge, rich market, and no one can deny, no matter how much they might want to, that the younger adult generation is inexorably moving into place as the dominant force on the planet and that the older people are just as inexorably getting older and fading from dominance. In the end, even the fact that the debate is hollow—a vigorous exchange of accusations and denial forming a façade behind which is nothing meaningful—is irrelevant: nothing can stop the transfer of power. All the *Newsweek* stories in the world, with their brightly colored boxes and neatly accumulated sound bites, will not make a blind bit of difference. Karen was right the first time, the Boomer era is ending fast.

The only thing that is really going to make a difference to all of our futures is how all of us deal with the worsening social conditions in America, and the hardening barrier between the haves and the have nots.

The problems are now so deep, there's no escaping them. When you realize that some impoverished families have been unemployed for *three generations,* you have to realize that for these people there is no possibility of the American Dream, only a tradition of hopelessness. Without hope there can't be morals; hunger and need and a sense of worthlessness chokes morality. Our ghettos have become cesspools of crime, spreading across the rest of society, because we aren't compassionate or smart enough to extend reasons for hope to people who must, eventually, if only out of self-preservation, take what they can't otherwise get. In the last twenty years, we've more than sold out our young, we burned our bridges too. Our policies—and our greed, and hypocrisy, and deceit, and our own amorality—have created a slice of humanity as scavengers, preying inevitably on us. Our much maligned young may be our last hope.

Bob Guccione, Jr.
Editor and Publisher
SPIN Magazine

1

How I Got Started

I accepted my dream job in November of 1989, after nearly seventeen years in the advertising business—Director of Media Services at McCann-Erickson, Detroit. It was not only a major agency in Detroit but one that boasted two (count 'em, two) divisions of General Motors among its client list. Running the media department (almost any media department) was the job I had secretly lusted after for years. But in truth it seemed unlikely for much of that time that I would ever get this kind of opportunity. Then, suddenly it was there, and I was anxious to make a mark.

I undertook the new position with what I hoped was convincing public modesty, and much private glee, since never before had a hometown woman risen through the ranks to become Media Director at a Detroit agency with a major automobile account. Certainly, I was the only Media Director I knew whose first job had been as a secretary. It was not that Detroit was "backward" as a city, I used to say; it was just that the advertising business here was dominated by the automotive industry, traditionally a bastion of machismo—Henry Ford, the assembly line, Hank the Deuce, the rust belt, the Industrial Revolution, John DeLorean, Lee Iaccoca, Ross Perot, and all that.

McCann's new *female* Media Director was a big deal, even in these semienlightened times. To give you an idea, in 1986, the Detroit Athletic Club voted to allow women full membership privileges for the first time in its history. In 1989, the Detroit Advertising Association (DAA), whose primary function was a monthly

1

summer golf outing, briefly threatened to disband over the same issue. The Adcraft Club of Detroit, the largest and most active advertising club in the world, has never had a woman President.

In this heady climate, the Detroit membership of the Woman's Ad Club enjoyed a season of unprecedented influence and, in their enthusiasm, elected me Ad Woman of the Year. Success was sweet. Little did I know that I was about to discover just how ignorant I was.

About that same time, the General Manager of our agency, a rather blunt-spoken, but friendly fellow named Jerry Atkin, came in to talk with me about the annual all-employee meeting. Traditionally, Jerry held a meeting in January of each year to assess for the employees the achievements of the previous 12 months. New accounts were listed. Awards were handed out. Information was passed along from Worldwide headquarters. In his typically understated way, Jerry called it the "State of the Agency" meeting. "Usually," he told me, "I ask the Creative Director to do the presentation. Show some commercials—something not too heavy—something all the employees can enjoy.

"But as you know," he said, "we just hired a new Creative Director, and he doesn't want to show the old commercials—they're not his work. . . . And he hasn't been here long enough to have new work to show. So I thought maybe it would be good to have the Media Director do the presentation this year, for a change. You could talk about new media technology, something like that. But don't make it too technical. Don't talk about cpms or anything like that. Remember, Todd the Mailboy won't understand that stuff. By the way, I think John Dooner and maybe Bob James will fly in for the meeting. So it's got to be really good. You can have all the A/V backup you need."

At that time, John Dooner was President of McCann-Erickson North America, and Bob James was Chief Executive Officer of McCann Worldwide. The assignment, as I understood it, was to write and deliver a presentation, on the subject of media, which would impress the two of them and Jerry and, at the same time, entertain Todd the Mailboy. The audience would include my new colleagues at McCann and everyone who now reported to me, but was actually still waiting to see whether or not I would fall on my face. Jerry was thinking about inviting reporters.

I considered early retirement. I considered hara-kiri, but this was Detroit. I considered asking the Woman's Ad Club to storm the gates with bras burning and placards in hand. None of these plans seemed foolproof.

At last there was no alternative but to face the challenge head-on. I decided to fall back on the tried and true. I reverted to what I had come over the years to call privately "the Baby Boomer trick." And once again, it saved me.

Throughout the '70s and '80s, I, like many other marketers, had learned how to take a quick initial read on the potential of a new product, a new media opportunity, or a new campaign by asking one simple question: Will Boomers like it? I had learned, as others had, that the sheer weight of this birth cohort we called Baby Boomers was often the difference between success and failure for a marketing concept. By analyzing the peculiar appeal of each new proposition to the leading edge of the Baby Boom generation, I could often predict which magazines would grow in popularity, which television plots would have broad appeal, and how to "grow a market" for a new product. It was as easy as it sounds. After all, leading-edge Boomers were my contemporaries. I only had to look about me—to observe my friends and relatives—and then to project what I saw to the larger population.

If the subject of my "state of the agency" presentation was media, I would simply apply the same yardstick. I knew that television had been catering to Baby Boomers for years. I would simply show how changing Boomer tastes were reflected in programming over the decades—how television grew and changed as Boomers grew and changed.

It promised to be a great show, if I do say so myself. I borrowed clips from *I Love Lucy* and *All in the Family* and still shots from the new television season. As I went through the history of Baby Boomers I was, I realized, also recounting the history of network television and the personal history of most of the McCann-Erickson executive group. Yet the twenty-year-old television footage was still entertaining for Todd the Mailboy and his friends—some of the jokes were still funny after all these years.

Then I got to that part of the presentation which dealt with the future. What could we anticipate, what was coming in the 1990s and beyond? And suddenly my old reliable yardstick failed me. I didn't know.

Oh, I knew that the leading edge of the Baby Boom would turn fifty in the '90s (as I would). I could predict a brief wave of nostalgia, as a large part of the population marked half a century. Indeed, we were already beginning to see it, and it was easy to choose examples from current shows like *The Wonder Years* and from magazine articles marking famous Boomer anniversaries. I could also predict a revival of the political activism that had characterized our adolescence. I was seeing that telltale restlessness among my own peers, as career goals were achieved and families grew up. My friends were looking for a return to "meaningful" activities, and volunteerism was enjoying a resurgence.

And, of course, I could predict great gains in technology. McCann was affiliated with the MIT Media Lab, and I was aware of new research into interactive television, electronic print, the latest in computer communications. I knew the breakthroughs, and their subsequent impact on the consumer marketplace, were closer than anybody imagined in 1989. But as I tried to visualize the face of the consumer of this new technology, his attitudes, his style of living, I came up blank. I knew the driving force of the new media marketplace would not be fifty- or sixty-year-old Boomers. We were trying to make our lives simpler. And most people over forty looked upon computers with all the enthusiasm of a ten-year-old facing a plate of boiled spinach.

No, the new consumer would be younger, raised with technology, hipper to electronics and computers than my contemporaries were. This new consumer was now in his/her late twenties or just turned thirty, and I thought, with no little chagrin, that I knew or had read or learned virtually *nothing* about people in that age group. What were we talking about here? People the same age as my children. How ludicrous! I was thinking about marketing to my own children. My God! It hit me like a clap of thunder: I was thinking about marketing to *Todd the Mailboy*!

I tried to fix the presentation. I searched for examples of products successfully marketed to young consumers. I couldn't find any. I looked for television shows whose popularity could be explained by their appeal to twenty-somethings. There were none. I looked

Todd Gilleland (Todd the Mailboy) was an early in-spiration to me.

for pictures of young people in magazines and found *not one*. Nobody looked even remotely like Todd the Mailboy.

I went with what I had. My "Baby Boomer" media presentation was good enough, so they let me keep my job. But I knew it wasn't good enough. Even as I concluded my presentation that day, I knew that I had not begun to attack what would be the core issue of the '90s: what comes after the Boom? I knew, even as I brazenly accepted the trophy as Detroit Ad Woman of the Year, that I was totally unprepared for the future of advertising.

During the next couple of years, I often found myself returning to this question. I was preoccupied with Generation X, but I was making little progress.

I would ask the young people on my staff about their interests and opinions. They seemed to find this amusing, but didn't tell me much that I could understand. I asked about their career goals. This was a concept that had inspired some deep thought. They would say things to me like, "You mean like earning twice your age? Goals like that? I would like to earn $50,000 by the time I'm 25. That's my goal. And also I want *your job*—that's my other goal." I couldn't get my head around it.

I read Douglas Coupland's book *Generation X*. I didn't get it, but I liked the name.

I noticed that there were fewer and fewer people on television who were in their twenties. Everybody in the media seemed to be aging.

I would try talking to my twentysomething daughters. I would say things like, "Wouldn't you like to have your own apartment?" Or, "Are you and what's-his-name thinking about getting married? Ever?" Or, "You can't start all over in college now! You just spent *ten years* in college. And what does one do with a degree in *botany*?" Things like that. They would say, "You don't understand. Things are different now." Or, "Get real, Mom!" Things like that.

I kept thinking that something was going to happen. Sooner or later, all these kids in their twenties or early thirties would catch the fancy of advertisers, and somebody would do a study. Sooner or later they would start to act in some predictable, understandable manner and we would then be able to make reliable predictions about the future of advertising.

I felt that this was important. My experience told me that people who were unacknowledged by advertisers and by the media did not somehow have the same advantages, the same visibility in our capitalist society. The media, after all, depicted our role models, our heroes. It taught us who and what to admire. If a group was ignored by the media, it was invisible in a larger sense to society as a whole.

During my own career, minorities had successfully campaigned to be represented in the media, because thoughtful leaders recognized that lack of such representation contributed to bigotry and prejudice.

Imagine for a moment, the public outcry if the networks were to announce that, in the new fall season, *Blossom* and *Married with Children* will be the only prime-time network television programs that would portray the lives of white people in America. . . . But if you can imagine how upset white TV viewers would be by a steady diet of narrow depictions of their lives, perhaps you can begin to understand why so many black television viewers are upset to hear news reports that the Fox Television Network has decided to drop *Roc, Sinbad,* and *South Central* from their fall lineup. . . .
—Clarence Page, June 12, 1994, *The Detroit News*

Blacks, Asians, and Hispanics wanted to be seen on television and to be acknowledged as consumers, because the alternative is to continue as an unacknowledged and persecuted underclass. When advertisers recognized that minority populations were potential "markets," they suddenly had "clout." And the desirability of these populations to advertisers helped them gain places in prime time, in daytime television, and on eyewitness news teams. Once there, stereotypes could be shattered and learning could take place on a broader scale. The desirability of these groups as markets, it seemed to me, contributed to their political and economic liberation.

Similar reasoning had inspired retirees, divorced or widowed women, homosexuals, and the physically challenged to regularly campaign for media representation and acknowledgment by advertisers. As a media buyer, I had been targeted by efforts from the American Association of Retired Persons, the National Organization for Women, and various other advocacy groups to help accomplish such recognition.

Still, Generation X stayed quiet. I kept waiting for somebody else to give me a clue. But nobody seemed very concerned about the younger generation. We called them "Baby Busters." We assumed they had no money. They told us they had no money. Everything stayed the same.

I went to Bermuda in 1992. I had been invited to speak at the American Magazine Conference, a convention of magazine publishers. I was one of a panel discussing the future of magazines—not that any of us had any special insights about what the future would be, but "the future of media" is a very popular topic with media people, and the panel was well attended.

I told the assembled publishers that I was puzzled by the media's continued emphasis on Baby Boomers. I told them that the media were ignoring younger people—Generation X. They were writing nothing that would interest people in their twenties, there were no programs on television that featured twenty-year-old characters, it was still difficult to find a photograph of a twenty-year-old in a major magazine. The consequence of this, as I saw it, was that the next generation would never look to the media as a source of information, entertainment and popular culture, the way Boomers had.

A funny thing has begun to happen lately, I said. Lately, when I look at my brother the Baby Boomer, I see a fifty-year-old man with a pot belly, a bald spot, and his own corporation. Yet, every day in our business we talk about reaching the younger Baby Boomer. What younger Baby Boomer? Face it. Boomers are getting old.

Perhaps, I said, it was time we started talking to the next generation: Generation X ... the purple-haired people ... Your kids, I said, and mine. You know who I am talking about, I told them. You probably have one at home. Maybe it was yesterday, you came home from work, and you found one of these purple-haired people lying about in your living room. And you looked at him or her, shook your head, and said to yourself, "I gave up drugs for this?"

I had hoped that my speech would have an impact, since these were issues that I found genuinely perplexing. But nothing had prepared me for the barrage of attention that followed. *Advertising Age* printed the text of my speech in its entirety. I began to get letters from young people across the country, I was invited by ad clubs and media groups and private companies to speak to them about Generation X, and I traveled from New York to Hawaii and from Oregon to Dallas, talking to marketers, listening to Boomers, and meeting Generation X in every city I visited.

November, 13, 1993

Dear Ms. Ritchie:

I am a part of Generation X. I read your article in November 9 issue of *Advertising Age* and discovered that so much of what you wrote rings true. But rather than being upset that the media has in a sense skipped my generation, I am thrilled.

It is nice not to have a plethora of magazine articles, television shows and advertisements aimed at me. . . . Please don't screw it up.

Sincerely,

Joseph B. Schramm

In no time at all the lemming effect had set in. In the past year, I've seen more articles about Generation X than freckles on a red-head. Most of these articles are slicker and more superficial than a Coke commercial, but at least we are finally talking about people under age thirty-five. At least we have finally admitted to ourselves that they exist.

In 1994, we finally see younger faces on television, we can occasionally read the opinions of young people in magazines and news-papers. If we don't always understand what we hear or read, if we don't always get it exactly right, at least we can say we are trying to communicate. Xers themselves are not always comfortable with this new scrutiny. After all, there is a certain safety in anonymity. But the recognition was long overdue, probably inevitable, and healthier, I think, than pretending that the Emperor is wearing new clothes.

> Now they're waking up to the discovery of 46 million people, which is like all of a sudden, noticing France.
> —Bob Guccione, Jr., *SPIN* Magazine, New York City

Finally, a brief word on the term "Generation X": Despite the fact that I have heard some objection to the use of this name, I have yet to discover a better one. I have not adopted Strauss and Howe's designation "Thirteener." Calling them by the number "thirteen" does not seem an improvement over the no-brand label. Similarly, *Details'* "Generation 2000" will lose its relevance in just a few years. More pejorative terms like Baby Busters, Slackers, or Latchkey Kids seem unfairly biased. The "MTV Generation" is self-serving and misleading (as was the "Pepsi Generation"). Attempts to glamorize them as "twentysomethings" or the "re-generation" have failed.

If it is any comfort, most Baby Boomers hate that term, too, al-most as much as they hated our other labels: Yuppies, Hippies, Yip-pies, and DINKS (Dual Income, No Kids). I actually prefer the term "Generation X," because it represents a group that has not yet named itself. There is also something anticommercial, antislick, anti-Boomer, and generally defiant about the "X" label. It is somehow specifically in your face, and at the same time hidden, like the generic brand, or the product comparison ad of the 1950s. It is mysterious, powerful, and a little threatening to the status quo.

One day soon, of course, they will name themselves. And that is how it ought to be.

2

Why Bother?

I didn't start this, you know. They did—all those people who started having babies at about the same time and raising those babies the way they did. Boomers may or may not be the literal parents of Generation X. More often the parents of those twentysomethings skip back to the "Silent" generation, the pre-Boomer group. But Boomers are the people who will have to deal with Generation X for the next thirty years, a circumstance that I believe has special implications for those of us in advertising and marketing. It won't be an easy relationship for either of us—Boomers or Xers—but we will manage, I think, mostly because we have no choice. Nevertheless, we should not underestimate the real generation gap that exists between us, for seldom have two successive generations had such basic differences.

I say this from the perspective of a Boomer with Generation X children, and as an employer with a Generation X work force. I say it from the perspective of a marketer, who realizes, at age fifty, that the world is a far different place than we thought it would be when we were young.

Marketers and advertisers and the media shall also have to learn new methods to cope with changing markets, because the facts indicate that the target market for most goods and services today includes a large number of adult consumers who belong to Generation X. At the same time, most of us who currently enjoy decision-making status as clients, agencies, or the media belong to

11

that legendary group called Baby Boomers, and that identification comes with its own unique set of baggage. Unless we understand that, unless we accept the fact that we are making decisions every day about people we may not understand—people who may not share our basic assumptions about the world, people whose life experience has been very different from our own—unless we understand that, we risk making mistakes that can cost us dearly.

Let us start by defining our terms. Historically, Boomers are defined by Landon Y. Jones (*Great Expectations*, 1980) and others as people born between the years 1946 and 1964, and so encompass that large bulge in the population that consists of children born after World War II. While most of us tend to accept this definition, the one we have heard throughout our working lives, it really doesn't work very well.

By this definition, I am not a Baby Boomer. Neither is Landon Y. Jones. He and I both missed being Baby Boomers by a couple of years, since we were both born in 1943. And yet, Boomers have dominated the world we live in for as long as we have lived in it. Landon felt strongly enough about Boomers to write a rather lengthy book about them.

I read his book, accepted his definition, and believed for many years that I was not a Baby Boomer. *And yet I have always felt like a Boomer.* Being a few years older doesn't matter. I have lived with Boomers and gone to school with Boomers and worked with Boomers my whole life. And for my whole life, Boomers have dominated the school system, the political process, the consumer marketplace, the job market, and the media from the time I was in kindergarten until this very day.

I identify with Baby Boomers. I have made my living selling products to them. As a student, I was inspired by their causes. I attended demonstrations. I wore bell-bottoms and let my hair grow long. I marched on Washington. As an adult, I still love rock and roll, and Gloria Steinem, and I still get a lump in my throat whenever I see the American flag sewn into the seat of somebody's blue jeans.

Still, according to what we've been told, the last Boomer (born in 1964) turned thirty in 1994, but how can it be that a Baby Boomer is too young to remember Vietnam, spent the "Summer of Love" in diapers, and the "Days of Rage" in first grade? These so-called "trailing-edge" Boomers do not identify with the Woodstock generation—they don't even remember Woodstock, except as one more silly story their parents tell.

Maybe the definition is wrong.

All marketers have witnessed the difficult, and sometimes ludicrous, attempts to make this definition fit the real world. We have ourselves struggled with various subdefinitions like "leading-edge" and "trailing-edge" Boomers. But, in our marketing souls, we know that the life experiences, thought processes, and product preferences of people born since 1960 are different from those of people born in the mid-1940s or 1950s.

For one thing, this huge birth cohort refuses to behave like a monolithic beast. When one tries to design a marketing strategy for a product with equal appeal to a forty-eight-year-old man and a thirty-year-old man, for example, one immediately begins to struggle. Today's young adult male is living in an entirely different life stage. Our forty-eight-year-old prospect is likely to be married and settled in his career. Our thirty-year-old prospect is more likely to be single and still struggling to make his first million. Both men fit the classic Baby Boomer definition, yet each is likely to have very different views about life, different taste in clothes, music, and cars, and different economic prospects. Therefore, while either man might conceivably be part of the target audience for a Buick LeSabre or a Chevrolet Camaro, we would not be surprised to learn that car-buying statistics indicate that the thirty-year-old is more likely to prefer the Camaro and the forty-eight-year-old more likely to prefer the LeSabre.

Could it be the way we advertise these automobiles? Perhaps we could reposition each product, feature younger men (or women) driving the LeSabre, hire a rock star to endorse the product, run ads in *SPIN* magazine. Many of us have lived through real-life campaigns that attempted just such ill-advised objectives. And, at the end of the day, no matter how many rock stars dance on the hood of a LeSabre, it is unlikely that the automobile will have any greater attraction for the average thirty-year-old.

Perhaps it is a function of the product. Let's imagine, for purposes of illustration, that we wish to sell more LeSabres to "younger Baby Boomers" so that, as our traditional buyers continue to age, we have new, younger prospects coming into our showrooms to replace them. Our target market is still adults 25–54 (like most automotive target markets), but our assignment is to attract the younger half of that demographic, without alienating the older half.

So we make certain modifications to the product: We make the LeSabre smaller and sportier. We retool the sheet metal, put the body on a smaller chassis, keep the engine large and powerful, add a stiffer, sportier suspension and a special steering package so the new LeSabre is quick and responsive. We eliminate certain luxury appointments, like dual temperature controls, adjustable seats, and leather trim, to keep the price low enough for entry-level buyers. We finish off with black-wall tires, neon paint, and blackout windows.

We have just designed a Buick LeSabre that will probably have strong appeal to "younger Baby Boomers." The only trouble with our hypothetical new LeSabre is that our traditional forty-eight-year-old prospect, the core of our Buick business for the past twenty years, doesn't like it any more. He wants his luxury back. He wants the greater leg room and head room and passenger-carrying capacity. After all, he has a wife and two kids and business associates, and he likes to go out to dinner on Tuesdays, and sometimes they take another couple along, and I am sorry, but this new, sporty car just won't do at all.

Suddenly, we have run head-on into a full-blown generation gap— a difference in lifestyle, attitudes, and life stage, which mandates a different product execution and/or a different marketing platform. As any marketer could tell you from his own experience, people born in the early '60s are different from older Boomers. Despite the fact that many advertisers use the demographic target adults 25–54, practical experience tells us that real adults tend to group more naturally into two age segments: over thirty-five and under thirty-five.

Most people between the ages of thirty-five and fifty will tell you they like rock and roll, but they can't understand (or they actively dislike) newer musical forms like rap or hip hop. Adults under age thirty-five like rock and roll, but they are also much more open to alternative music.

If you are under thirty-five, you may sometimes choose rum as your alcoholic beverage. If you are over thirty-five, you probably have not tasted rum in years. Likewise, if you are over thirty-five, you are more likely to drink Scotch; if under thirty-five, you may never drink it. If you are over thirty-five, you grew up watching network television and you still tune to those network channels first, even though you may watch less of them than you used to. If you are thirty-five or younger, you grew up with more choices, and while you watch a lot of television, you incorporate cable and syndication and video in a much more interactive way. When is a Baby Boomer not a Baby Boomer? When he/she doesn't act like a Baby Boomer. In other words, when he or she was born later than 1960.

Many "thirtysomethings" share some characteristics of Boomers (as do many people over fifty-five), but as a group, those under thirty-five more closely resemble their younger brothers and sisters, in basic lifestyle and attitudes. At the same time, people like me, people born from 1943 through 1945, have more in common with Baby Boomers than with the "Silents" who preceded the Boom. The life experiences and product consumption patterns of people born after the start of World War II are not terribly different from those of people born a few years later.

Under most circumstances, a product that appeals to a man in his late forties also seems to make sense to a man in his early fifties. Buick LeSabres sell comfortably to adults over the age of thirty-five, while virtually none sell to younger adults. If you liked Scotch when you were forty-five, you probably still like it when you are fifty-one or fifty-two. And, as we all know, Mick Jagger continues to rock and roll well beyond his fiftieth birthday.

In retrospect, one has to wonder that the definition of the term "Baby Boomer," has remained unchallenged for so long. Perhaps we instinctively believe that the concept of Baby Boomers is right. It feels right, it works for us—it has always worked for us. It just doesn't work as well around the fringes.

This is true in virtually every consumer product category. And it is not just a matter of life stage. If it were only life stage that made the difference, then today's twentysomethings would be driving Volkswagens, wearing beards, getting married, and listening only to rock and roll—they are not.

In their book *Generations: The History of America's Future 1584–2069*, William Strauss and Neil Howe propose that a generation be defined as "a cohort group whose length approximates the span of a phase of life and whose boundaries are fixed by peer personality."[1] The definition has two elements. The first is the length of a generation: in general parlance, this is the length of time required to produce offspring—the next generation. Because people tend to have their children at different ages, and because those children tend to marry other people whose parents may have been younger or older than their own parents, our definition of a generation must be flexible enough to accommodate all possible combinations of parents and children. Strauss and Howe propose a complex matrix which sets the length of each life phase at approximately twenty-two years, with adjustments for historical circumstance. This results in a new generation every eighteen to twenty-four years.

Strauss and Howe define Boomers as those born between 1943 and 1960. Even though this definition slightly shortens the length of the Baby Boom (to eighteen years, from nineteen), it is immediately and instinctively more satisfying. The Strauss and Howe definition is inclusive of those people who, like me, were born during World War II, but it excludes people, like my daughters, who were born in 1961 or later. Thus, Strauss and Howe include old rockers like Mick Jagger and Janis Joplin, who were formerly considered too old to be Boomers. Steve Martin, Angela Davis, and Oliver North also join the Boomer ranks, while Michael J. Fox, Eddie Murphy, and Whitney Houston belong to Generation X.

Generation X, called "Thirteeners" by Strauss and Howe, because they are the thirteenth generation produced in America since its founding, are defined as born between 1961 and 1981, inclusive, a twenty-one-year cycle. I have used the Strauss and Howe birth year matrix to define Boomers and Xers throughout this book, and I believe it represents a major advancement in our understanding of both generations as major agents of social change.

The first consequence of this new definition is its effect on total population numbers for each generation. Using birth years 1943 through 1960, the number of Boomers alive in 1995 is approximately 69.5 million—a huge number, but significantly smaller than the 75 million Boomer noses counted in earlier texts using birth years 1946 to 1964. Note that the 1990 census count represented the peak of Boomer population. After that year, emigration fails to equal anticipated deaths, and total Boomer population begins a slow and steady decline.

Using birth years 1961 to 1981, Generation X accounted, in 1995, for 79.4 million people. That is correct—there are *more Xers than Boomers*, and there have been since about 1980. So the first Boomer myth is exploded. They can no longer claim to be the largest generation ever produced in America. (See Figure 2–1.)

Figure 2–1
Total Population
Xers vs Boomers

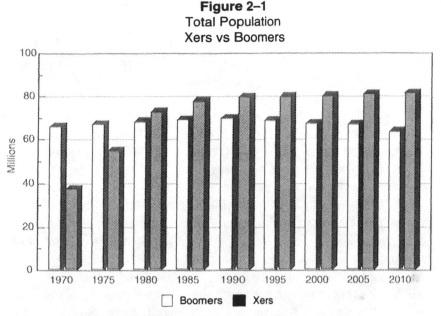

Source: Statistical Abstract of the U.S. 1991

The second element that defines a generation is "peer personality," and it is this aspect which most concerns us as marketers or advertisers. Peer personality consists of patterns of behavior and beliefs that are dominant among a group of people born during the same period of time. Not everyone in a peer group will adhere to these patterns (not all Boomers love rock and roll), but even those who march to a different drummer, will recognize the patterns as dominant. (Rock and roll is here to stay!)

The peer personality concept is an important one, especially as we seek to understand marketing to this new generation. I will plead guilty to stereotyping—a certain amount of stereotyping is probably unavoidable. Of course, I acknowledge that not all Baby Boomers are alike. Nor will all Xers recognize themselves in these pages. But each generation shares with its peers a common history, and living that history has in some way defined the world for us so that we mutually understand who we are and how we fit.

If Citizen A was a paratrooper in Vietnam, and Citizen B marched in protest, while Citizen C waited out the war in Toronto, these facts *mean something* to Boomers. Vietnam is part of our common history, and we understand these cues.

Generation X doesn't define itself in relation to Vietnam. They are too young to remember Vietnam, so the same facts about the activities of Citizen A, B, or C in the distant '60s carry few, or none, of the same emotional cues for them. If one is too young to remember the war in Vietnam, one is too young to recognize or relate to a significant aspect of the Boomer "peer personality." On the other hand, if you were born between 1961 and 1981, chances are that you or your peers suffered some trauma while growing up, as a result of crime, guns, drugs, or all three. Boomers may be concerned about crime in the streets, but as children, they were not confronted by the everyday reality of kidnapped/missing children, drug wars, armed robberies in grade school, drive-by shootings, and teenage suicide. A Baby Boomer may recall the school bully who made his young life miserable, but chances are that he did not feel his life threatened in the same way that Generation X did.

If you remember Vietnam as one of defining events of your life, while the War in the Gulf was a minor skirmish, you are probably too old to be called Generation X. If, on the other hand, some of your friends served in the Gulf, and you are not really sure what made Vietnam such a major deal, when people die on the streets of American cities every day, you are definitely not a Boomer.

Since the end of the Vietnam War, that country has produced its own Baby Boom. Understandably, now that some measure of peace and stability has returned, the Vietnamese have returned to having and raising children. Harm du Blij, geography editor of *Good Morning America*, reports that sixty percent of the population of Vietnam is now under the age of twenty.[2] In the simplest terms, more than half the population of Vietnam today is too young to remember the war. "The War," the event that rocked the social conscience of our "best and brightest" generation—that so divided our own country, it is only within the last five years that we could begin to openly acknowledge its impact. We Boomers are still troubled in the aftermath of Vietnam. Yet today, most young adults in the country where it happened do not personally remember it.

It is not a surprise that Xers have passed Boomers in numbers. What is surprising, even amazing, is that until very recently, it

Figure 2–2
Generation X as Percent of
U.S. Poulation

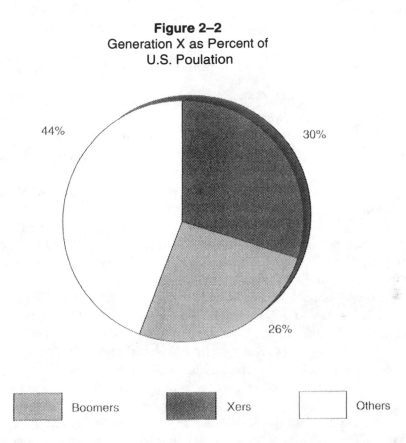

44%

30%

26%

| Boomers | Xers | Others |

seemed nobody had noticed. In 1995, Generation X accounted for 30 percent of the total U.S. population—nearly one out of three people—and yet they remained virtually invisible to marketers (see Figure 2–2). By contrast, Boomers in 1995 made up a noisier 26 percent of U.S. population and continued to hold center stage in the hearts and minds of American commerce. As Boomers continue to age, advertising targets continue to creep toward older demographic groups. In the early 1980s advertisers actively sought to reach adults and women 18–34. In the mid-'80s the emphasis shifted to adults and women 18–49, and as we enter the mid-'90s, many advertisers still track Boomers, now targeting adults 25–54.

In the sixties, "the win" was about experimentation and protest. In the seventies, it was sex, drugs and rock'n roll. In the eighties, it was easy to keep score. "The win" was highly visible. It was all about career, money, and material things.

The question now: How will boomer men define "the win" through the nineties?

—Media Sales Brochure for *Men's Health*, 1994

Note the age of most celebrity spokespersons, whether it is Merlin Olsen selling flowers, Robert Urich for pet food, or Candace Bergen for Sprint. Skippy Peanut Butter continued to use aging Mousketeer Annette Funicello as its primary spokesperson through the early 1990s. Hardy's Restaurants featured Regis Philbin and Joan Rivers in 1994 commercials, while Denny's competed for share of mind with the charismatic Corlick sisters.

Coca-Cola, the soft drink that was marketed in the 1960s as "the choice of a new generation," launched the nostalgic "Always Coke" campaign in 1993, while Pepsi ran a series of commercials in 1994 themed around the woodstock reunions.

Clothing manufacturers, even those noted for trend-setting chic, also play it safe. DKNY targets Boomer women in the pages of *Vogue* and *Mirabella*. The Gap advertises in *Town & Country*—median age of reader, 41. Kid-targeted Kudos share the pages of *USA Weekend* with Crisco shortening and prostate treatments.

In 1994, domestic and import car manufacturers fielded three models targeted to the over-thirty-five buyer, for every model targeted to younger buyers. And the September 1994 issue of the *Reader's Digest* featured Chrysler on the second cover and Ford on the third cover.

The Fox Television Network, which originally flaunted its appeal to 18–34 audiences over the older, traditional networks, announced with the 1994 upfront season that it would introduce new programming to attract a broader (older) demographic set. Fox, like other young-skewing media, had found it difficult to sustain enough advertising support with their Generation X audiences alone.

The median age of the average magazine's audiences increases about a year for every year the book is published, as editors cater to established markets and fail to attract younger readers. The typical daily newspaper reader is now so old that a general alarm has been raised in the newspaper industry, and publishers are scrambling frantically for ways to increase readership, while despairing the lack of a literate constituency.

There is nothing intrinsically wrong with making cars or peanut butter for older buyers, but we have always been taught that sheer numbers equal impact on the marketplace. In the words of Landon Y. Jones:

> The size of a cohort is the force that shapes its life. . . . The size of a generation is its most crucial characteristic.[3]

Generation X is the largest generation we have produced in this country to date. If, as commonly stated, Boomers represented a critically important market *simply because there were so many of them*, then why is the same logic not commonly applied to Generation X? Why do we perpetuate the "leading-edge, trailing-edge Boomer" mythology, instead of questioning such an awkward marketing definition? Why don't we recognize Generation X as a larger, younger cohort just approaching the age of influence in the marketplace? Why, instead of devising new products and services to appeal to young adults, do we spend nearly all our marketing energies trying to sell blue jeans and soft drinks and sporty cars to middle-aged target audiences?

The answer may be that Boomers have developed a peculiar blindness to Generation X. This oversight has arisen partly from a natural desire to think of themselves as young, and from an instinct to preserve their own hard-won base of power. In a way, Baby Boomers have held the franchise on youth in America for the past fifty years and may find middle age a more difficult assignment.

Of course, we like to think of Boomers as young, because if Boomers are no longer young, then I must be fifty years old. Well, the truth shall set you free, dear reader, but first it is going to piss you off. Baby Boomers were young when Kennedy was elected. It has taken them more than thirty years to finally elect a president from their own ranks. No wonder they often feel as if they are just starting to get somewhere.

Boomers are, in fact, just coming into their golden age. They now hold most of the top and midlevel corporate and government jobs. They earn the largest salaries, own the most expensive houses, wear the best clothes. They run the banks and the media. Boomers are rich and powerful, but this does not make them young. The truth is that the fortunes of Baby Boomer marketers have been directly tied to the fortunes of the Baby Boom generation for so long that they may have begun to lose perspective. In the following pages, we hope to reestablish some of that perspective.

Baby Boomers also tend to overlook Generation X precisely because they are younger. While they represented one of three U.S. citizens through the early 1990s, they were only one out of four U.S. adults (see Figure 2–3). Since many marketers and the media tend to target and to program for adults (age 18+), the Generation X phenomenon will mature in about 1995, when Xer adults will nearly equal Boomer adults in number.

Another reason marketers have been slow to acknowledge Generation X is that many marketing futurists have been less than enthusiastic about the prospects of this group. Watts Wacker, of Yankelovich Partners, Inc., did probably the greatest disservice of all when he labeled them, in the late 1970s, as "the first American generation who will not do as well as their parents."[4] *The Yankelovich Monitor*, a syndicated research survey of the American consumer, attempts to measure emerging trends, attitudes, and beliefs and has been a tool used by major advertisers and their agencies for over twenty years. *The Monitor* has been a strong bellwether of the changing marketplace for major advertisers. So when

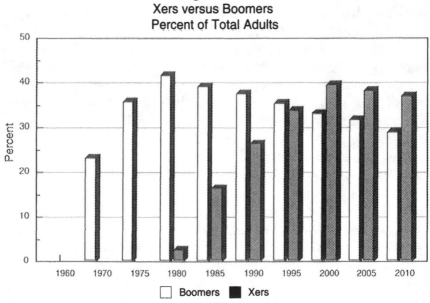

Figure 2–3
Xers versus Boomers
Percent of Total Adults

Source: Statistical Abstract of the U.S. 1991

Yankelovich first began to report the behaviors and attitudes of an emerging new peer group, the impact of Mr. Wacker's statement upon marketing plans throughout the country was profound and long-lasting.

Many advertisers accepted the prediction that the so-called "Baby Buster" generation would never achieve the level of affluence enjoyed by Boomers and wrote them off as a prospective market before the first wave had finished high school.

Then came Strauss and Howe, first in *Generations* and then in *13th Gen*, continually stressing Generation X's lack of access to the American Dream:

> LISTEN UP, DUDES! Where earlier twentieth-century generations could comfortably look forward to outpacing mom and dad, you'll be lucky just to keep up. When you marry, you and your spouse will both work—not for some Boomerish self-fulfillment, but because you *need* to, just to make ends meet. . . .[5]

In 1993 and 1994, most articles written about Xers stressed their limited prospects. Not only were Xers believed to be fewer in numbers but it was also predicted that they would be less affluent and, therefore, less desirable to advertisers of all stripes. This fashionable belief had little basis in fact and is one of the issues addressed in the following chapters.

In late 1994 we also saw a spate of articles suggesting, incredibly, that Generation X no longer exists. As if in the '90s, life had accelerated to such a pace that an entire generation could appear, mature, reproduce itself, and die out, in the space of a few short years. No, I don't think we get off that easily. The pace of life may be quicker, but it still takes seven years to lose your baby teeth.

Rather, there is another, more subtle reason that Generation X has been overlooked and undervalued, and that reason is intrinsically bound up in the Boomer peer personality.

Boomers, including Boomer marketers, are addicted to center stage. They have occupied that place for their entire lives and are not ready to abdicate in favor of a group that clearly rejects so many of their core values and beliefs. At their core, Boomers are idealists, who sincerely believe that the ideas they subscribe to are more important than the comfort or welfare of other people. We have seen examples of this throughout Boomer history, as time and time again they have disturbed and disrupted the status quo in favor of an idea. Throughout their lifetimes, Boomers have not hesitated to interrupt official government ceremonies, bring turmoil to national political conventions, and disturb major cities and small towns from Mississippi to Los Angeles, on behalf of civil rights or to draw attention to the war in Vietnam. They disrupted college campuses and high school classrooms to demonstrate for various political causes, marched, picketed, sat in, sung in, and loved in, at recruitment centers, power plants, and abortion clinics without regard for tradition, or for the feelings, beliefs, or sensitivities of those who opposed them. It is, in fact, this streak of blind idealism which has made Boomers such effective agents of social change.

But while idealism and a strong sense of self may be charming traits in an individual or group, these same traits in an advertiser can become inflexibility and smug self-satisfaction—potentially fatal flaws in today's competitive marketing environment. The first time an advertiser says to the buyers of his product/service, "I know better than you what's good for you," that advertiser takes the first giant step toward obsolescence in the marketplace.

Boomers used to know this. Boomers have always prided themselves on their ability to effect social change. They have, in fact, changed the business of marketing and advertising—they have made it more accountable, more scientific. When Boomers were young, they used statistical analysis and strategic planning to coax or coerce an older management to take a chance on them. Older clients feared alienating customers with more traditional values. But Boomers convinced them that the world would not end if they advertised in *Ms* or *Rolling Stone*, if they associated themselves with rock and roll, or *All in the Family*, or *The Smothers Brothers*.

Boomers were successful marketers. They sold cars to women, when some thought it couldn't be done. They sold laundry soap and prepared food to men. And their success grew. They put black and Hispanic and Asian faces in commercials and showed young hippies singing on mountaintops, and marketing to Boomers became one of the most lucrative initiatives an advertiser could undertake. Boomers were so successful in marketing to other Boomers that *now they don't know how to do anything else.*

Here in the '90s, a peculiar stubbornness has set in. I, for one, find it extremely ironic that the generation whose anthem was "sex, drugs, and rock and roll" has emerged in middle age as one of the most repressive and reactionary generations this country has ever produced. The same people who invented free love and LSD now won't let me smoke a cigarette within twenty-five feet of corporate headquarters. The same people who campaigned so vigorously for equal representation and compensation for women in the workplace are now arresting women for leaving their children unattended while they go to work. They proclaim an ethic of "New Traditionalism" and the triumph of "family values," in an economic environment that *requires* two paychecks to maintain a decent standard of living.

The same folks who grew their hair long, did drugs, and dropped out now shake their collective heads in mass despair when one of our children shaves his head and refuses to accept one of the "low-pay, low-prestige, low-dignity, low-benefit, no-future McJobs" (as Douglas Coupland said in *Generation X*) left unoccupied by Baby Boomers.[6]

What we have here is a real and growing inability to communicate. Most of "us" are Boomers—idealistic, manipulative, flashy, and headstrong. We have things to sell to "them." Our livelihood rests on our ability to sell "them" products, and services, and ideas, and television shows, and jobs in our industry. But they are Generation X—streetwise, once-burned, pragmatic, and suspicious. Our energy is met with apparent numbing lethargy and indifference. Our conviction is matched with impregnable skepticism. Our charm eludes them. They don't get the jokes, they don't take us seriously, and they don't think this is funny. All our sure-fire strategies fail us now. They just don't cut any ice with these new audiences. How do we begin to reach a generation which, in Coupland's book, cries out, "I am not a target market?"

3

What Did We Do to Deserve Them?

L et's begin at the beginning. In 1995, Generation X numbers 79.4 million people, about 65 million of them adults. Their age ranges from fourteen to thirty-four years. By the next Census, there will be more Xer adults than Boomer adults living in the United States. The population of Generation X adults will continue to grow at an average rate of approximately 3.6 million each year, until the year 2000. By the year 2000, there will be 79.8 million adult Xers, ranging in age from nineteen to thirty-nine years.

In 1995, they represent about half the demographic target, adults 18–49, and about 30 percent of adults 25–54. (See Figure 3–1.)

As a group, they have denied themselves little in the way of personal luxuries. They are well traveled. They are as likely as Boomers to have purchased a new car—and almost as likely to prefer an imported car. Relative to their numbers, they buy more CDs, drink more cola, consume more fast food, and smoke more cigarettes than Boomers do.[1] As their numbers grow, Generation X will become the majority of the market for these goods.

Relative to their numbers, they bought more disposable diapers, gas ranges, oven cleaners, and electric can openers than Boomers bought in the past twelve months. As more Xers move into their thirties, more will marry, and their new households will require new appliances, new furniture, and all those household goods that line the shelves of our supermarkets.

Xers are 50 percent more likely than the average U.S. adult to par-

Figure 3–1
Generation X
Percent of Common Target Audiences (1995)

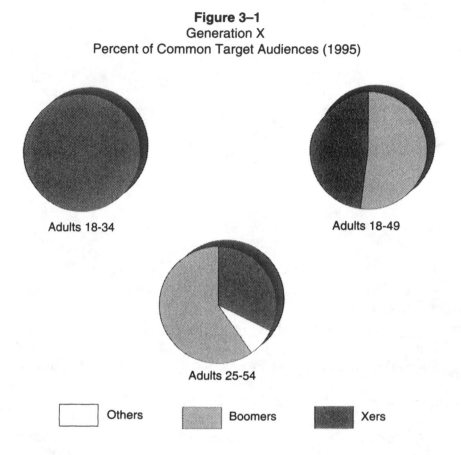

Adults 18-34   Adults 18-49

Adults 25-54

Others   Boomers   Xers

ticipate in aerobics, 10 percent more likely to be a member of a health club, and slightly more likely to have visited a resort/spa in the past twelve months. They are major consumers of health and exercise equipment sports equipment and clothing for sports and leisure.

According to most syndicated research, Xers represent a good market for cameras, for clothing, for most cosmetic products, and for certain kinds of financial products. They use more creme rinses, gel, and mousse than Boomers do. They drink more beer and wine coolers, and they are the volume consumers of rum, tequila, and vodka. They use more toothpaste, chew more gum, wear contact lenses more often, and play more video games. In virtually every product category, Xers are an important part of the present-day market and are unquestionably the market of the future.

But Generation X is different in some fundamental ways from the Boomer market advertisers have come to know and love in the past. To a large degree, these differences arise from a different historical perspective. The familiar world to Generation X has little in common with the world that gave birth to the Baby Boom, and even events that are experienced by both groups in common are likely to have been experienced from vastly different life stages and circumstances.

In order to understand just how Generation X is different, it will be necessary to briefly review what we know of the Boomers' life experience.

As children, Boomers benefited in a manner like no generation in America before or since: from an all-consuming drive toward homogeneity. After the trauma of two world wars and extended separation from home and family, all that young parents wanted to do in the 1940s and 1950s was kick back, get normal, and grow kids and a lawn—activities they immediately undertook in historic numbers.

Boomer children, as a group, enjoyed a safe and child-centered family life, the image of which still has a strong hold on their collective psyches. It is ironic that, having been nurtured in that homogeneous environment, Boomers have since spent their lifetimes challenging and dismantling the very institutions that made their own childhood so apparently idyllic: They have championed the rights of the individual over the institution, revising, in the process, our expectations of the educational system, liberalizing the media and the government, and changing the fundamental structure of the nuclear family unit. It is an irony not lost on Generation X, who must sometimes wonder why Boomers worked so hard at tearing apart the social fabric that was good to them. From Robert Lukefahr, aged twenty-nine co-editor of *Diversity and Division*: "Drugs, the deficit, a bankrupt political system, bad schools were the legacy boomers gave us—and now they blame the victim."

What Generation X may not know, and what we may have failed to make clear, is exactly how far the pendulum had swung by the mid-1950s toward national conformity and away from individual expression.

Life under those circumstances was often stultifying, and those who did not or would not conform were, at best, uncomfortable and, at worst, persecuted by the majority. Black, Hispanic, and Asian

Americans suffered institutionalized segregation and harassment ranging from discrimination to lynching. There was no place in the homogeneous American 1950s for Communists, homosexuals, single mothers, or radical politics. The "traditional role of women," for example, was narrowly defined as that of homemaker and mother.

It was commonly believed by marketers during the '60s and '70s that families of the 1950s were typical of the American family throughout history, and that the mothers of the Baby Boom were somehow the prototype for American Motherhood. In truth, marketers were mistaken about that.

There was a related belief that young Boomer women were somehow flying in the face of history (and perhaps tempting fate) by deserting more traditional roles and flaunting their newfound independence. This was likewise a false alarm.

In fact, Baby Boom women represented in many significant ways a *return* to the norm, rather than a radical new direction. Baby Boom women actually had more in common with their grandmothers than they did with their mothers. As Steven McLaughlin says in *The Cosmopolitan Report*, "It was the mothers of the Baby Boom, rather than their daughters, who departed from historic trends."

Sorry, Beaver, but it was your mother, Mrs. Cleaver, who was in reality one of a statistically aberrant group of women—women who married earlier, divorced less frequently, had more children, and withdrew from work and education in a way that no American women have done, before or since.

Most people are familiar with the huge increase in fertility rates that initially gave rise to the so-called "Baby Boom." What is less well understood is that this increase in fertility did not represent the norm in the pattern of fertility for U.S. women—either before or after it occurred. In *The Cosmopolitan Report*, Steve McLaughlin traced the pattern from Census information dating back to 1922:

> The total fertility rate has been declining for 200 years with minor fluctuations. The only significant exception to this overall pattern was the baby boom—the rise in fertility during the 1950's to levels not seen since very early this century. *Current fertility patterns represent a return to previous historic trends.*[2] [emphasis mine]

If one compared the fertility rate in 1977 to that in 1957 (as many marketers did), one might be convinced that Americans were

Figure 3–2
Total Fertility Rates in the United States
1922-2010

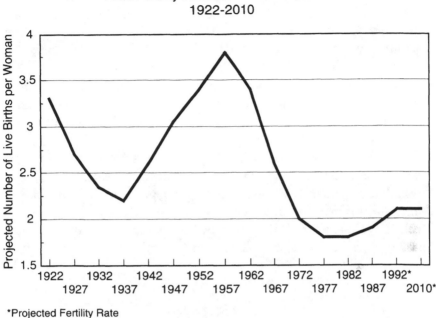

*Projected Fertility Rate

Source: Cosmopolitan Report "The Changing Lives of American Women" (1986)
Statistical Abstract of the U.S. 1991

headed toward extinction as a race. (See Figure 3–2.) But, in fact, we can trace a gradual reduction in fertility rates from the early part of the century through the early '40s. If the mothers of the Baby Boom were removed from the data, we would see the fertility rates in the early '70s simply pick up at the point where we would have been had the trend been uninterrupted.

The number of children they bore was not the only characteristic that distinguished the mothers of the Baby Boom. They also married at a younger age, had their first child at a younger age, and divorced less often. As a result, they spent a larger percentage of their lives as married women and mothers.

Even more significant in its effect on their economic prospects, the mothers of the Baby Boom spent less time in formal education and less time working. Until the 1940s, American women were educated at about the same rate as American men of the same period.

For example, in 1900, the percentage of women who had one or more years of college was just slightly less than the percentage of men who had completed the same level of schooling. In the years just after World War II, however, the G.I. Bill allowed young men a significant advantage in financial aid for college. This financial incentive, coupled with the newfound emphasis on home and children, caused women's educational attainments to fall behind those of men for the first time since the beginning of the 20th Century (see Figure 3–3). As a result, the mothers of the Baby Boom found themselves doubly disadvantaged in the job market.

Similarly, it was common during the 1950s for women to drop out of the work force during their childbearing years. The pattern was that a woman typically worked after graduating from school, until she got married, at which time she would retire to pursue her role as "homemaker." If a woman continued to work after marriage, she would almost certainly stop working when she began to

Figure 3–3
Percent Completing One or More Years of College
Men versus Women

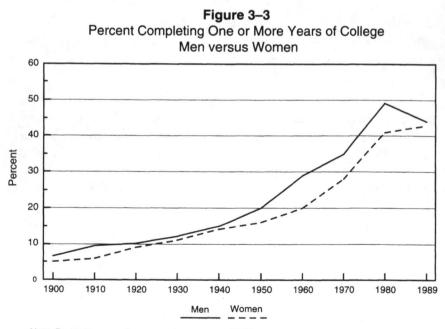

Note: Percentages are for men and women age 24-29

Source: Cosmopolitan Report "The Changing Lives of American Women" (1986)
Statisical Abstract of the U.S. 1991

Figure 3–4
Working Women by Age
1950 versus 1990

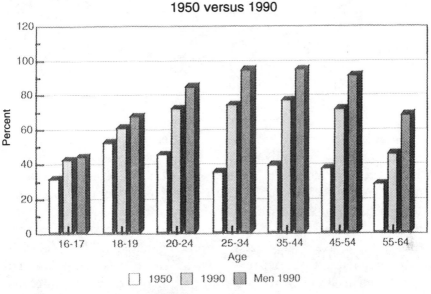

Source: Statistical Abstract of the U.S. 1991

have children. This pattern was so well accepted that many employers *required* a pregnant woman to leave her job, and some careers (airline stewardess, for example) required that a woman be unmarried. This form of blatant discrimination continued in some places well into the late '60s.

Because of boredom or economic necessity, some women would return to the work force later in life, usually after their children were grown. (See Figure 3–4.) But by then most women were unlikely to have acquired any significant level of work experience, and whatever skills they once possessed were certain to be terribly out of date.

A 1950s *man*, on the other hand, entered the work force with a higher educational level and then continued to build up a pattern of work experience in his chosen profession over the course of a lifetime. The "quality" of the female work force in America, as expressed in education and work experience, began to decline significantly as compared to the male work force.

There were other factors that contributed to keeping women out of the workplace. There was an overt bias toward men, who were regarded as "breadwinners," while women were regarded as dependent by nature. This bias was so strong that it simply ignored the fact that some women were themselves "breadwinners." They were simply regarded as aberrant or unusual cases. The attitude was especially prevalent in the years following World War II, when it was considered a patriotic duty to hire a veteran, even if a woman was displaced to make room for him.

Young women were routinely "guided" by public and private schools into socially approved curricula like "home economics" and guided away from math and science. Women were often harassed and discriminated against in the workplace.

But the real villain standing between women and economic independence was the declining quality of the work force. It became a self-fulfilling prophecy: Women did not expect to work and did not prepare for careers. Because women were not prepared for careers, they did not have them. Because women generally did not have careers, women did not expect to work. And it was this downward spiral which Boomer women later confronted as they became adults and went to work.

The fact that Boomer daughters overcame their mothers' abdication of the workplace is a tribute to their spirit and tenacity. During their lifetime, Boomer women broke down virtually every existing barrier, from level of skill to inbred discrimination, to establish themselves as a qualified and competent work force. In doing so, they confronted and reversed a decades-old orientation toward American women, which defined them by their familial roles. They became, rather, primary individuals, independent of their family status. It is perhaps their most significant achievement.

In the 1990s a woman's typical lifetime work experience looks much more like a typical man's experience in continuity and seniority. Today 53 percent of all undergraduate degrees and more than half of all masters degrees are awarded to women. In 1960, women earned about 5 percent of all M.D. degrees and less than 3 percent of law degrees. Less than thirty years later, women earned one of every three medical degrees, and more than forty percent of all law degrees (see Figure 3–5).

Thus today, the quality of the female work force is similar to that of the male work force. Equal pay and equal access to the executive suite are inevitable, and just a matter of time.

Figure 3-5
Percentage of Degrees Awarded to Women
Selected Professions 1960-1990

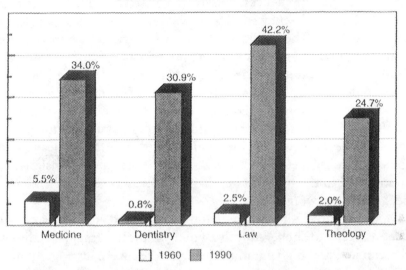

Source: Statistical Abstract of the U. S. 1993

But these gains for women in the workplace did not come without cost, most notably in the increased tension between the demands of home and the demands of work. We are only now beginning to question the price paid by Boomer women in terms of personal sacrifice and time spent away from their families.

Meanwhile, young Boomer men had their own problems. Throughout the '60s and most of the '70s, children, family, and the rights of women were probably not uppermost in the minds of most Boomer men. The country was at war until 1973, and Vietnam was a critical concern for most draft-age men. If Boomer women were expected to become dependent housewives, Boomer men were expected to be voluntary cannon fodder.

The prolonged war in Vietnam cost the Baby Boom its head start on the good life as adults. For some young Boomer families, the War complicated life, interrupted educations, and delayed the start of business or professional careers. For some, it was a life-changing experience, which took years of recovery. For others, it was literally the end.

No matter where one stood on the issues, the choices that faced us in regard to Vietnam were not easy ones. Any decision had real life-changing consequences, and the debate lingered long after most of the troops had returned. There was no clear or easy resolution of the conflict. The soldiers who fought remained burdened for years by our national embarrassment over Vietnam. Those who protested were often criticized and sometimes persecuted by families, employers, and government agencies. The discord continued for years, even after we tried as a nation to put the War behind us.

The aftermath of Vietnam included national and individual trauma, drug dependency, unemployment, and political upheaval. For some Boomers, these factors also exacerbated family tensions and contributed to the breakup of marriages as often as did the new independence of women.

Boomers moved, therefore, from a childhood that was generally safe, secure, and sheltered into a young adult life fraught with danger, conflict, and high emotion. Because they were large in number, and because they were creative and self-confident, Baby Boomers were able to overcome the trouble they confronted as young adults, transforming themselves and the rest of society in the process.

It is impossible to guess how much of the creativity and self-confidence that have marked this group can be attributed to the fact that, as children, most Boomers enjoyed two parents who stayed married to each other and a mother who was home when they needed her. There are those who credit this common 1950s family structure as ideal for producing healthy children, strong marriages, and happy families. Nevertheless, Boomers did not follow the example of their parents when it came time to form their own families.

How different life was for Xers! Most were born during a period of our history when birth control was suddenly cheap and available. It was, therefore, not particularly fashionable for them to be born at all. Unlike the mothers of the Baby Boom, whose lives were presumed to revolve around home and family, the mothers of Generation X had a lot more to deal with.

On the downside of the Baby Bulge, we see a precipitous drop in the birth rate beginning in about 1960, and continuing to 1975—the very years when our Xers were being born. (See Figure 3–6.)

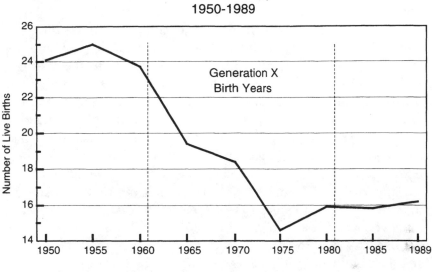

Figure 3–6
Birth Rate Per 1000 Population
1950-1989

Source: Statistical Abstract of the U.S. 1993

The smaller number of babies reflected the advent of the birth control pill and, as noted, restored the U.S. birth rate to a more historically normal pattern. It was also this pattern which originally inspired the term "Baby Busters" and represented the first derogatory, and misleading, label for Generation X.

When Xers arrived, their mothers were already significantly challenged—finishing their education, working at entry-level jobs, caring for a household, and preparing for a lifelong career. Working mothers had less time and energy for the children, and the 1960s career woman had few resources to tap. By 1987, when the youngest Xers entered the first grade, we had 12.4 million kids in day care. But for older Xers, safe and convenient day care was in scarce supply. Most of what was available was private at-home care (babysitters), reserved for the preschool child. Once of school age, a child with a working mother was frequently on his own between early school dismissal and whenever mother got off work. There were no "latchkey" programs, since working women with children were still considered aberrant and exceptions to the normal order.

Often children went home alone or with siblings or other relatives. Sometimes a neighbor or relative could be relied on to "look in" on young children, and sometimes not.

The additional stress placed on the family by the tension between home and work meant that something had to give, and despite the '60s rhetoric, it wasn't going to be Dad to the rescue—which simply added to the conflict surrounding Xer children. If Boomer mothers hoped for greater paternal involvement, Boomer fathers were slow to respond. Even when willing to defend a woman's right to equal pay and equal access, many men still failed to acknowledge the unequal distribution of responsibility in their personal relationships. Child care was still considered woman's work, and that did not change, even when married women had full-time jobs. For the majority of families, this issue did not begin to move toward resolution until the 1980s, and some will say it has not been resolved today. Still, Generation X continued to be born, and their mothers continued to work. (See Figure 3–7.)

Throughout the 1960s and 1970s, young mothers tried to bal-

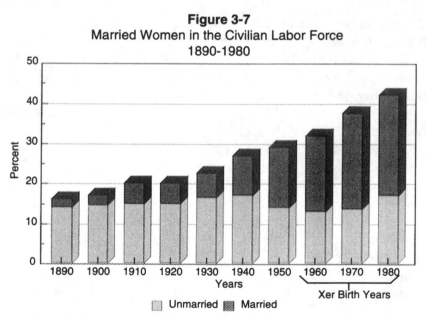

Figure 3-7
Married Women in the Civilian Labor Force
1890-1980

Source: Cosmopolitan Report "The Changing Lives of American Women" (1986)

Statistical Abstract of the U.S. 1991

ance the traditional demands of home and family against the requirements of their equally demanding new careers, all the while seeking to redefine their role with few reliable guideposts. Because Mom was less able to manage the housework and cooking, and because Dad was unlikely help, household chores in many families fell to Generation X children, who learned at an early age to feed themselves, to navigate the supermarket, and to operate household appliances. When something had to give, it was often Generation X who handled repairmen and deliverymen, who amused themselves and their younger siblings, who did the dishes and put the dinner on. While earlier generations had undertaken similar household chores, Generation X was perhaps the first that undertook them alone, and in such large numbers. A Boomer child may have "helped Mother with her housework," but Generation X had full responsibility and vastly fewer resources. With parents away, and often far removed from the aunts, cousins, and grandparents of the rural extended family, Xers learned cooking and shopping and child care on their own.

In retrospect, it is easy to see the first seeds of the Generation X peer personality in this childhood experience. While some Xers resented the responsibility, others rose to the occasion and learned to take pride in their own resourcefulness and independence. Both sets of attitudes survive today in many Xer adults.

The Generation X child was also witness to (and sometimes victim of) newly coined concepts, like "quality time," "supermom," and "open marriage." He was, by now, getting hard to convince that new catchwords made life better. He watched as parents, teachers, friends, and older siblings sought to deal with life's increased complexity—as coping mechanisms of dubious quality, like "I'm OK, you're OK," the new math, astrology, scream therapy, and recreational drugs, each had a span of popular support and were ultimately supplanted by a newer fad.

As young children, Xers sometimes found themselves cast in the role of responsible party, pragmatically scrubbing the bathroom or warming up a pizza, while the adults in their lives searched for meaningful solutions, contemporary role models, or pots of gold. This was especially true when divorce entered the picture.

Not all Xers have divorced parents, but Generation X is twice as likely as Boomers to be the children of divorce. The rate of divorce per 10,000 women more than doubled from 1955 to 1975 and remained high throughout Xer childhood years. What 1950s children referred to as a "broken home" became so common among Generation X children that the stigma formerly attached was completely gone by the mid-1970s. Everyone, it seemed, knew someone whose parents were divorced, and few of Generation X were completely untouched. (See Figure 3–8.)

"Perhaps our single most common characteristic is our nearly universal exposure to divorce," says Steven Gibb, Xer author of *20-Something: Floundering, and off the Yuppie Track* (Fawcett). "We have a general lack of models to teach the grace of marriage."

If divorce taught them little about grace, it taught many Xers a great deal about poverty and financial insecurity. Even comfortable, middle-class families saw the split-level floor drop out from under them when Mom and Dad called it quits. For families already struggling to make the house payment, divorce could mean real financial ruin. The price tag of the escalating divorce rate fell disproportionately on children who largely remained with their mothers—mothers who were paid less than men, and who seldom collected regular child support payments.

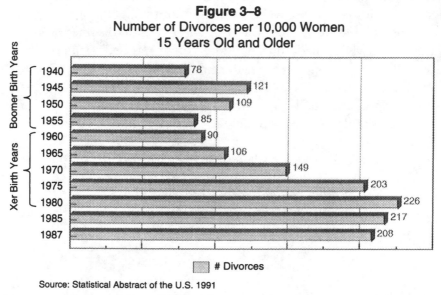

Figure 3–8
Number of Divorces per 10,000 Women
15 Years Old and Older

Source: Statistical Abstract of the U.S. 1991

Cosmopolitan Report "The Changing Lives of American Women" (1986)

The number of children living below the poverty level increased steadily, peaking in 1983 (when the last of Generation X was just two years old) at more than 13 million children. Two out of every three of these poverty-ridden Xer children lived in a single-parent household.[3]

It was not necessary for every Xer to personally experience divorce in the family for the concept of divorce to have a profound effect on the entire group. Divorces were occurring among their friends and relatives. The financial consequences were often clearly visible, as friends and relatives were called upon to help the abandoned and the destitute. The emotional impact was also apparent, as young Xers lent support to friends the same age as themselves, as they listened to stories and circulated gossip. Divorce occurred on a large-enough scale to the disruptive to the security of the entire Generation, and to help form their earliest opinions about marriage, family, and trust.

Later, as divorced parents remarried or single-parent households struggled to cope with financial difficulties, the nontraditional family unit became more commonplace. The new family was less rigidly defined and might include grandparents, half-siblings, roommates, stepchildren, lovers, and housekeepers, in all sorts of new combinations.

Where an earlier generation turned to "sex, drugs, and rock 'n' roll" to help deal with teenage angst, Generation X went to work. It made sense: Work gave them a measure of independence. They didn't have to ask Mom when they needed a few bucks, and it got them out of the house for extended periods of time. Also, they were used to working and used to being on their own.

They started working in high school, or sometimes in grade school, and wasted no time after graduation in lining up a full-time job. Those who went to college worked summers, after school, between classes, or on the weekend. As Strauss and Howe report, "Theirs is the biggest child labor generation since the days of turn-of-the-century newsboys and garment girls. The high school students of the '80s and '90s are working longer hours for pay (after school and during summers) than any previous generation in American history."[4]

And if Xers were insecure before they entered the job market, what they encountered when they got there made them crazy: corporate downsizing, higher tax rates, increasing government regulation, and the transition to a service-based economy. As Boomers hit it big in the affluent '80s, Xers toiled for long hours in fast-food restaurants and learned the true meaning of minimum wage.

The stagnant state of the American economy over the past decade has confirmed their worst fears about staying afloat on hourly wages and sent them flocking toward higher education in record numbers. (See Figure 3–9.)

In contrast to the stable nuclear family unit that nurtured most Boomers, the Generation X family was often characterized by new or unusual family composition, evolving roles, conflict, broad swings in affluence, and a never-ending stream of new babysitters. As a result, the generation has developed a unique perspective on marriage and family—a point of view that is at once more flexible and less idealistic than the perspective of earlier generations.

Generation X is much more inclusive and less rigid in their definition of "family" than even liberal Boomers were. The Roper Organization reports that Generation X is 86 percent more likely than Boomers to agree "There is no single right way to live." And *De-*

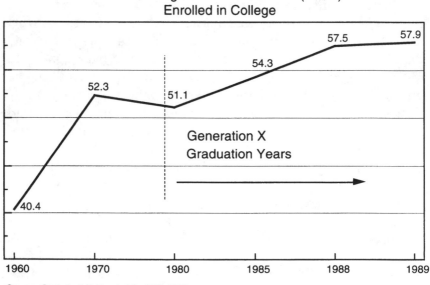

Figure 3–9
Percent of High School Graduates (14-24)
Enrolled in College

Source: Statistical Abstract of the U.S. 1991

Figure 3–10
What Constitutes a Family?

	Percent Xers Who Agree
A family is any two or more people who love and take care of each other	71
A single mother with a child can be considered a family	70
A gay or lesbian couple with children can be considered a family	46

Source: Details Magazine National Survey 1993

tails magazine found Xers to be much less traditional in their ideas about what constitutes a family (see Figure 3–10).

Boomers helped to expand and to destigmatize our somewhat narrow definition of family to include previously disenfranchised people like single mothers and children of divorce. Generation X, often themselves the sons and daughters of divorced parents, expanded the definition even further. Boomers initiated the rhetoric, but Generation X bought the underlying principles.

At the same time, Generation X is clearly cautious about taking on the responsibility of marriage. As a group, they are less likely to marry in their twenties than Boomers were (see Figure 3–11).

The increase in young singles is particularly striking. In 1992, more than half of adults 18–29 had never been married. And according to *Newsweek*, 46 percent of single twentysomethings are still living with Mom and Dad.[5]

If you ask, most Xers would say that they prefer to be out on their own but cannot afford it. In fact, there are at least four reasons why Generation X has delayed coming out.

First, they are insecure about their future and cautious about relationships. Many are simply taking their time before committing to marriage and family. Some cite this as a natural reaction to parental divorce. Others believe that marriage should be for life and, therefore, should not be undertaken lightly. Generation X,

Figure 3–11
Single Persons (Never Married) Age 20-29
Percent of Population

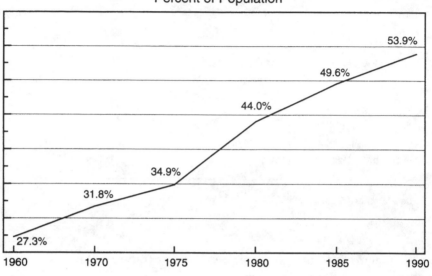

Source: Statistical Abstract of the U.S. 1991

like their Depression-era grandparents, are chronically plagued with economic anxiety. And who could blame them? Whether at home or in the job market, Xers faced one potential economic disaster after another in their personal lives. Very little of what was forecast was optimistic for their earning potential, as Boomers threatened to hold all the top jobs through 2020.

The second reason Xers don't leave home is that they are under relatively little pressure from their Boomer parents to move out. The '90s are not the '50s, and Boomer parents are more "broad-minded," and under less financial pressure, than their own parents were. They are less likely to encourage premature marriages or uncomfortable career choices. They also recognize that young adults are social and sexual beings, and there is less pressure to conform to rules of conduct concerning sexual abstinence, drinking, smoking, and the like. It is also socially acceptable for Boomers to have adult children at home, since so many families are in similar circumstances.

Further, as we have noted, many Boomer parents, myself included, were unable to spend uninterrupted time with their children when they were growing up. Divorce and/or work kept many of us from being with our children the way we wanted to when they were young. Once those children are grown and require less maintenance, we like to have them around, perhaps to remind ourselves that we are a family after all.

The third reason that Xers stay at home is that living at home allows many to cope with poor economic prospects without sacrificing their taste for luxury. Perhaps in less affluent families, the "boom or bust" quality of multiple marriages and career changes taught the children that "rich is better." In more affluent circles, Boomer parents frequently substituted "things" for the personal attention they had as children. Too busy to share themselves with their children, they gave them toys instead. In any case, the result was surprisingly similar: We have raised a generation who have come to regard life's little appliances as "necessities" and whose idea of "roughing it" is to have the VCR in for repairs. Generation X consequently aspires to a far higher standard of living than Boomers ever did. And many, when confronted with a choice between subsistence-level independence or life with mom and dad in relative material comfort, will choose the car, the basement apartment, the high-tech stereo, and the color television over moving out on their own.

Bradford Fay of the Roper Organization, agrees that the gap between expectation and reality has been a significant pattern for Generation X:

> The ethos of the 1980s was an expectation of prosperity at little cost to government, business, or to individuals. As a product of these years, the expectations of Generation X grew dramatically. Indeed, they grew much faster than their ability to realize their dreams, leading to huge letdowns in the 1990s.[6]

Finally, because the women of Generation X do not necessarily expect to be supported by their husbands, they are under less financial pressure to find a husband early, before all the "good ones" are gone. Indeed, many Xers of both sexes view marriage as a compromise to financial independence and want to be sure that it is worth the sacrifice.

When Generation X does decide to take the plunge, their marriages may be very different from those of any generation that has preceded them. Generation X may be the first generation in America in which women have truly equal status, and the basis is economic.

Much of the concern about this generation's economic potential has been based on the analysis of men's wages. American productivity stagnated in the early 1970s, and on the average, the growth in our standard of living had slowed through the end of 1993. Strauss and Howe have observed that this economic "flattening" has not affected all groups of workers in an equal way—that the wages of young men have grown the least of any demographic group.

This is true. But while young men's wages have been growing more slowly, women in all age cells except the oldest have profited more than men. According to the Bureau of the Census' *Current Population Reports*, women still make considerably less than men on the average, but the gap is narrowing, as women's wages increase faster than men's wages in almost all age cells.

Earnings that in other decades might have gone to young male workers were disproportionately redistributed to women workers. Women aged 25–34, working full time and year-round, earned 62 percent more in 1989 than in 1980. Men's wages in the same age group increased by only 41 percent—a 21-point advantage for women. The bad news is that Generation X men have lost ground economically. The good news is that Generation X women are making up for some of those losses. (See Figure 3–12.)

In the 1990s, the two-income household is an economic necessity, and the responsibility to provide for oneself and one's children is no longer assumed to be the sole province of men. Generation X women are as well educated as Generation X men. They expect to earn equal pay for equal work. And they understand that if they expect to enjoy the comfortable lifestyle that is their aspiration, they must work, and earn, right along with their husband or partner.

In spite of much of the angst expressed in the popular press, and by Xers themselves, about working mothers, most Generation X women seem resigned to work, and most Generation X men expect that their wives will work. When *Details* magazine commissioned a survey of the attitudes of Generation X, they found only one out of four Xers agreed that "young children suffer when the wife works outside the home," and only 22 percent agreed that "I would like a traditional marriage where the wife stays home."[7]

Even when they agree *in principle* that it is better for a mother to

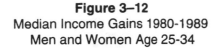

Figure 3–12
Median Income Gains 1980-1989
Men and Women Age 25-34

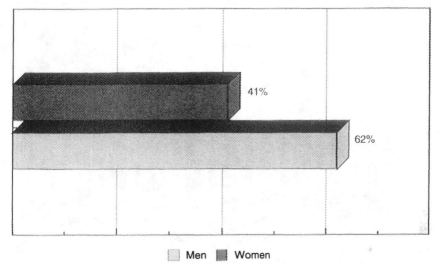

41%

62%

◻ Men ▨ Women

Source: Statistical Abstract of the U.S. 1993

be at home with the children, few Xers expect such an arrangement in their own marriages. Perhaps they are simply being pragmatic about the cost of living and the necessity for two incomes in the modern household. Then again, perhaps as children, watching the women in their lives struggle so hard and so long for the sake of their career or to raise themselves out of poverty, Generation X gained an appreciation for the importance of work in the lives of women.

Whatever their motivation, Generation X women expect to work, and start working early in their lives. In 1991, 50 percent of women 16–19 years old were working at paying jobs, up from 31 percent in 1960. And women's work force participation shows no sign of slowing down as Generation X reaches adulthood. Among Xers, half of all college degrees go to women, as compared to 46 percent of all Boomer college degrees, and today, there are almost as many women in the work force as men. (See Figure 3–13.)

Most Generation X men expect their wives to work, and many prefer not to be the sole source of income for the family. But, hav-

Figure 3–13
Civilian Labor Force
Distribution by Sex

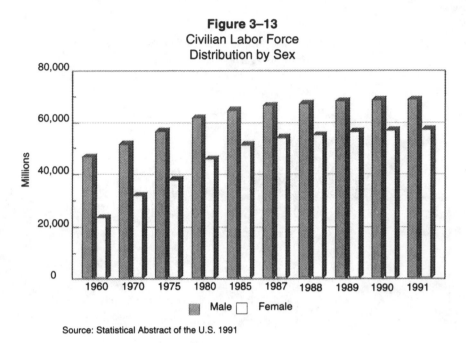

Source: Statistical Abstract of the U.S. 1991

ing been raised with working mothers, they seem to have a more realistic grasp of what is required to make a household run. Both men and women agree that housework and child care are not the exclusive province of women. More than 80 percent of Xers surveyed by *Details* agreed that "I expect to share house care and child care equally with my spouse or partner."

In return, Generation X men may not feel that supporting the family is their responsibility alone. In most young households today there are two wage earners to provide some cushion when illness or other calamity interrupts the family income. And having two wage earners often allows a family to afford both the necessities and some discretionary purchases that a single wage-earner would be hard-pressed to provide. Since many Xer men are not strangers to the vacuum cleaner, helping with the housework seems to them an acceptable tradeoff.

Generation X men have also been encouraged to experience all the trials and satisfactions of raising and educating their children—an experience that had been reserved for women for decades. Many are not at all intimidated by the prospect, and some have embraced it, even when their wives have abdicated the responsibility. Here the future is uncertain, but as two-income families continue to make the inevitable compromises, it has become more common to see a father patiently coping with small children at the supermarket or wiping a runny nose on the way to school. Single-father households increased by 73 percent from 1980 to 1989. While still not huge in number, single fathers are no longer the oddities they once were.

We sometimes hear that stay-at-home mothers are fashionable again. *The Wall Street Journal* reported in October 1993 that in certain more affluent communities, a stay-at-home wife has become a new sort of status symbol. Throughout the early '90s, *Good Housekeeping* proudly described its core readers as "the new traditionalists." However, none of the data supports a major movement of American women away from the workplace. What these trends suggest instead is an attempt to restore some balance between work and family and a move to consolidate the gains made by earlier generations.

4

Diversity Reigns!

Naming is power, but power from nomenclature most squarely rests with the name givers—in this case, not us. What's worse, once we were duly noted, we were supposed to be duly notable. But this generation is so dis-unified that the only thing that could be said about us all in the context of this contrivance was that we were lost, confused and alienated. So nam-ing us was as oxymoronic as putting a bunch of hermits in a room and la-beling them "loners."[1]

Generation X is more diverse—ethnically, culturally, and econom-ically—than any generation that has preceded them. Today, the number of white non-Hispanics is less than 75 percent of all Ameri-cans and is projected to represent a declining percentage of the U.S. population well into the year 2020. By that year, non-Hispanic whites will comprise about 64 percent of total U.S. population.

But, depending on where you live in America, racial diversity can be a much larger factor in your daily life. In six of the largest U.S. metropolitan areas, the gross total of blacks, Hispanics, Asians, and others exceeds fifty percent of the total population. (See Figure 4–1.)

In ten other large cities, racial "minorities" comprise more than one-third the population. (Note that these numbers are not strictly additive. Hispanics may be of any race.) (See Figure 4–2.)

When recent emigrants are factored in, especially people whose language or culture may be significantly different but whose race does not identify them in census data as a minority (Moslems, Indi-ans, Chaldeans, etc), the "majority" population gets even smaller. Detroit, for example, which is known for its large black popula-tion, is also home to the largest community of Arab emigrants out-side the Middle East.

In California, more than a fifth of residents are emigrants, the high-est percentage in the nation. And U.S. Immigration and Naturaliza-

Figure 4–1
Largest Metropolitan Areas
Race and Hispanic Origin Population: 1990

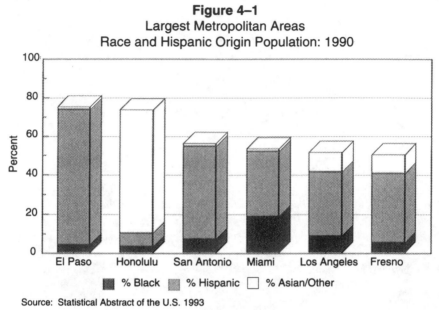

Source: Statistical Abstract of the U.S. 1993
Note: Percents not additive. Hispanics may be of any race.

Figure 4–2
Largest Metropolitan Areas
Race and Hispanic Origin Population: 1990

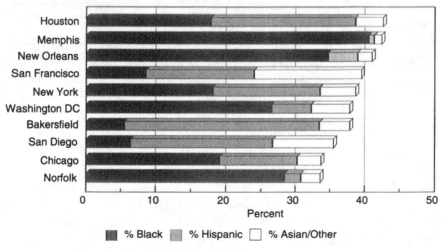
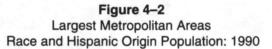

Source: Statistical Abstract of the U.S. 1993
Note: Percents not additive. Hispanics may be of any race.

tion estimates that between 3.5 million and 5 million illegal emigrants currently reside in the United States, half of them in California.

The U.S. Bureau of the Census anticipates a continued gradual decline in the birth rate for all Americans. But the birth rates for whites will continue to be dramatically lower than for blacks, Hispanics, Asians, and others. As a result, the white population in America is older than other ethnic groups, and this age gap will continue to increase over the next thirty years. By 2020, the median age for whites will be forty-two, ten years older than blacks, and twelve years older than Hispanic Americans. In America, the younger you are, the more you encounter diversity among your peers. As a result of all these factors, the white American of European descent, who was assumed to be the majority of the Baby Boom generation, may well be a minority in Generation X. (See Figure 4–3.)

Protection of the rights of minorities is a founding principle of American government, and one that is especially effective when the minority population is large, well organized, and vocal. But, in Generation X, everybody is a minority.

Figure 4–3
Projected Median Ages of U.S.
Racial/Ethnic Groups

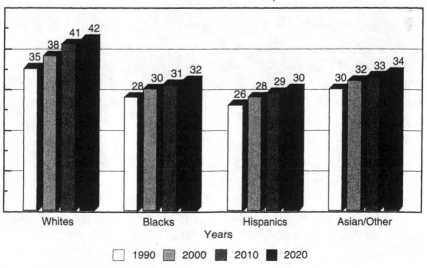

Source: Statistical Abstract of the U.S. 1993

According to *Business Week*, we have seen a significant decline, in the past ten years, in the percentage of white male professionals and managers in the work force. These jobs are increasingly being taken by women and/or minorities.

> Through the year 2005, the Labor Department estimates that half of all labor force entrants will be women and more than one-third will be Hispanics, African Americans, and those of other races.[2]

The years 1993 and 1994 saw a continuing spate of reverse-discrimination lawsuits, principally filed by white men who asserted that they had been wrongfully dismissed or who had lost a job opportunity to a woman or minority candidate. In most cases, these suits have been unsuccessful. It has been difficult, given the preponderance of white men in the top-level executive suites, to convincingly position them as an oppressed minority.

So with their traditional slice of the American pie getting smaller all the time, many white male Xers have had to revise their expectations for opportunities in education, business, and the professions. In the Boomer generation, a middle-class white man of mediocre talent and limited credentials might have expected, as part of his natural birthright, a college education, followed by a comfortable, midlevel berth in a 1960s corporation. But the Generation X white man faces too much competition to take anything for granted—another of those disparities between expectation and reality that have contributed to the general anxiety level of Generation X.

> He hasn't selected any colleges yet, but Curt Harms is concerned about the impact of diversity on his chances for acceptance. "I'm worried," says Harms, a 15-year-old sophomore from Lake Bluff, Ill, who is white. "If there's a candidate who has grades and credentials exactly the same as mine, these days it's more likely they'll take that person over me, if the person is a minority or a woman. There's nothing I can do.[3]

At the same time, blacks, Hispanics, and others may find that their opportunities in the contemporary business marketplace actually exceed their expectations. The percentage of managers and professionals who are white women increased from 37 to 42 percent between 1983 and 1993. And, as companies like IBM, Corning, Honeywell, and others embrace diversity as a corporate goal, talented minority candidates will find themselves "fast-tracked" toward executive row, perhaps faster than they believed possible.

And that can create its own brand of stress. As ground-breaking Boomer women can attest, a minority pioneer may find that jealousy, peer-group hostility, a lack of role models, and institutionalized condescension are part and parcel of the road to success in business.

> If I use my own "slang", that's too ethnic. If I play golf, that's too white. Anytime you go outside the box you are wrong. . . . It's hard.
> —Cynthia Doty, Detroit

Xers also live with a greater economic gap—a greater difference between the "haves" and the "have-nots"—than has previously existed. It would be a mistake to assume that racial diversity and poverty are directly related. Even though blacks and Hispanics are disproportionately represented among the ranks of the poor in America, not all the poor are black or Hispanic. Instead, we see greater division within every group—regardless of ethnicity. The rich are richer, whether they are black, white, brown, or yellow, and the poor are homeless.

Blacks currently represent 12 percent of all Americans and will grow to over 13 percent by 2020. Geographically, black Americans are concentrated in the southeastern United States and in large metropolitan areas. The "hot spots" for future growth are the outer-ring suburbs, where non-Hispanic blacks continue to improve their economic status and continue to press the gains of the civil rights movement. In large metropolitan areas, the average income of suburban black families is more than $32,000—55 percent higher than the average for black families in the central cities, according to *USA Today*.

The largest concentrations of Hispanic populations are in the west and southwestern parts of the United States, as well as in south Florida. Hispanics currently represent 9 percent of Americans, but that number is expected to grow nearly 40 percent over the next ten years. By 2015, Hispanics will outnumber blacks in America. In some large U.S. cities, like Los Angeles, Miami, and Houston, Hispanics already outnumber blacks. Hispanics are also the youngest of all population groups, with a median age of twenty-six.

But these statistics can be misleading, since all Hispanic Americans do not share the same cultural heritage, national background, or language. (See Figure 4–4.)

Nor are Hispanic Americans equally assimilated or equal in terms of their economic and political clout. In some regions, most notably southern Florida and parts of Texas, Hispanic Americans play a major role in local businesses, schools, and civic matters. Their influence is growing, as Hispanics increasingly represent these regions in local and national political organizations.

Indeed, 60 percent of all U.S. Hispanics live in California, Texas, or Florida. Cuban-American businesses are central to the economic base of Miami and other cities. The Spanish language and culture

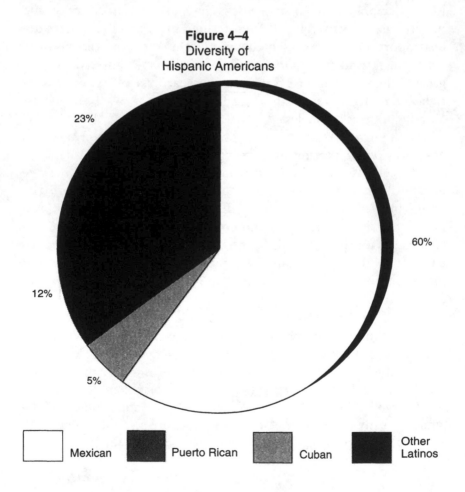

Figure 4–4
Diversity of
Hispanic Americans

are essential elements of public life in Los Angeles, San Antonio, and parts of New York City. In northern or midwestern states, like Maine, Michigan, or Iowa, however, this is not the case, and Hispanics are more truly minorities in the northeast.

As a group, Hispanics have spending power. According to a new report from DRI/McGraw-Hill, Hispanics now spend well over $200 billion a year on goods and services. While Hispanic households in the United States have a lower median income than non-Hispanic households, 13 percent of Hispanic households have incomes above $50,000.

Asian Americans are the fastest-growing minority group. Asians have both a relatively higher birth rate and a high rate of emigration. As a group, they increased in number by 108 percent from 1980 to 1990 and are expected to exceed 17 million people by the year 2010. Like Hispanics, Asian Americans are not a monolithic culture, but represent very different languages and cultures, including Chinese, Filipino, Japanese, Indian, Korean, and others.

Asian American households are relatively affluent, according to a study prepared by *USA Today*. One-third have incomes of $50,000 or more (compared to 29 percent of white households), and they are better educated than the average American: 21 percent have completed four years of college, as compared to 13 percent of all Americans.

Boomers grew up in an atmosphere of racial intolerance. In fact, the process of breaking through that intolerance, the dismantling of institutionalized racial segregation, and the championship of civil rights in the '60s and early '70s were additional markers of that generation. Many Xers, by contrast, understand the hard-won access to racial and sexual equality as a given. In most cases, their environment was racially diverse from childhood. Most Xers did not have to grapple with the struggle for racial integration.

At the same time, Xers of all races experienced, up close and personally, the conflict, tension, and friction of a newly integrated United States. Some Xers learned bigotry and racial hatred at home, but were required by the new legal reality to ride buses, attend integrated classes, and learn new codes of conduct in public. Others were raised in households with liberal values, but lived in homogeneous neighborhoods and seldom encountered individuals of another race. Most Americans accepted the new standards and tried to get along with other races. But Generation X (white, black, or brown) recognized from an early age the difference between the ideal and the reality in race relations.

White Xers, in particular, often do not value the accomplishments of the civil rights movement in the same way that their parents do. In many ways they are more tolerant than Boomers ever were, and in other ways, they have less patience with the differences between groups of people. Daily interaction and competition in real-life situations have often highlighted the friction between races and ethnic groups, rather than the cooperation. In general, Generation X has learned to live in a multicultural society, but Xers are also aware that tolerance has neither eliminated all our prejudices nor solved all our societal problems.

> Another stereotype is that Generation 2000 is generally open-minded and socially liberal because they were raised with greater diversity and multiculturalism than previous generations. While a liberal bent may be reflected in their abstract philosophies, in practice this generation espouses fairly traditional values, and remains relatively suspicious of those who are perceived as "different."
> —Skip Pollard: Details Magazine

Aware of the prevailing climate of politically correct behavior, some Xers, particularly those in large multicultural cities like New York, simply wrap themselves in indifference, believing it the best way to avoid confrontation. They disguise their feelings with neutral expressions and adopt the posture, "You don't bother me, and I won't bother you." In some segments of the population, racist sentiments have simply been driven underground, to flare up in occasional street corner or night club confrontations. Most Xers hate the tension, but see the nuances of diverse racial interaction with great clarity. Hugh Gallagher commented on the MTV hip-hop program *Yo! MTV Raps*:

> How long is hip-hop going to stay confined in its hostile urban sets while the white rockers prance carefree through verdant, breathtaking scenery? The channel is time-slot segregated and dominated by white acts. Latinos and Asians are nearly nonexistent, almost all hosts are white. Black music gets a minimal slice of air space, except when it's being used in the background of fashion ads where white women

prance across the screen, setting the standard of beauty. Riots are imminent on MTV unless programming is changed, and I don't think there's much of a doubt that *Yo!* could kick the whole channel's ass if a full-out broken-bottle brawl busted out.[4]

In a national survey of Generation X conducted by *Details* Magazine, 37 percent of those interviewed said they were "a lot more comfortable with people who have come from backgrounds like mine." Less than half (48 percent) said they had close friends of different races or ethnic groups.

One-third of Generation X (38 percent) said they would be comfortable dating a person of another race or ethnic group, and an equal number strongly disagreed. One out of four (26 percent) said they could see themselves marrying a person of another race or ethnic group, and two out of four (48 percent) strongly disagreed.

It should be noted that, while these numbers may fall short of the ideal for a multicultural society, they reflect a huge move toward tolerance in a single generation. A generation ago, people were beaten and lynched for interracial dating. In the '50s and '60s, interracial couples were so rare that they attracted enormous attention in most public places. Interracial couples were never seen on television. The responses of Generation X in 1993 reflect both a strong element of pragmatism and an enormous movement toward tolerance.

Each ethnic group will, of course, bring a different perspective to the issues:

> I'd like to be a slacker, but my family would kick my ass. A poor Mexican worrying about esoteric emotions like angst? Get a job, *mijo*.
> —Lalo Lopez in *Next*

Julianne Malveaux points out that, because of the civil rights movement, Boomers of African-American descent bonded more closely with their own parents. ". . . there is not as sharp a generational divide between black boomers and our brothers and sisters from the so-called silent generation."[6] As a result, black Boomers continue to share power, more or less comfortably, with older black leaders. Black Boomers rebelled less against their own parents and family traditions (as white Boomers did) and more against the repressive system.

As black Boomers worked to consolidate and safeguard the gains of the '60s, they were often content to let these older leaders remain in the spotlight, while they themselves carved out careers, seeking economic opportunity and better lives for themselves and their families.

> While the generational changing of the guard in the White House also resonates in the African American community, such a transfer of power has yet to be realized in the institutions we control or have major influence over. Witness the age of those African Americans who head civil rights organizations. . . . Even black big-city mayors with the longest tenure are long in the tooth—like Los Angeles's Tom Bradley, 70, and Detroit's Coleman Young, 74.
>
> The Clinton administration may have chosen more whites from the boomer generation for Cabinet and other key leadership positions, but the blacks it has reached out to—from advisors like transition chief Vernon Jordan and children's advocate Marian Wright Edelman to appointees like Energy Secretary Hazel O'Leary and Commerce Secretary Ron Brown—have more often been from the silent generation. . . .[7]

There is no question that the civil rights movement has been a force for unification in black America. Common goals have transcended generational differences. But as the economic gap between black achievers and the black disenfranchised continues to increase, there are signs that this unconditional unity may be weakening. Middle-class blacks who have worked hard to achieve a better life find themselves increasingly impatient with issues of drugs and crime that continue to drag down the whole society. In the central cities, hard times continue unabated. Generation X "gangsta rap" artists flaunt guns and threaten violence against women, whites, cops, and "Uncle Toms" alike. Black-on-black crime has reached such epidemic proportions in the central cities that the Rainbow Coalition, headed by Jesse Jackson, convened a national conference in early 1994 to confront the issue.

Black Boomers, who lived through the '60s and saw both the positive result of the struggle and the distance still to travel, cannot help but feel sympathy and rapport with blacks still trapped in the cycle of poverty and hopelessness that characterizes life in too many of our central cities. At the same time, the black and Hispanic middle class now has a stake in the system—a stake gained after long struggle and often at great cost. It is unlikely they will abdicate it now to lawlessness, gang warfare, or crime.

Those young blacks and Hispanics who have assimilated into the middle class now find themselves thrust into a pluralistic society that still finds it difficult to accept them as full equals. At times, the gangsta rappers reflect their own hostility and the frustration of their own ambition. At the same time, educated middle-class minorities recognize that the serious threat to societal order postulated by the genre of young, tough gang members threatens them as much as it threatens their tormentors. Young, middle-class blacks and Hispanics, perhaps more than any other segment of Generation X, suffer daily the obligations of the past and the uncertainty of the future.

Even as American blacks and hispanics seek to manage second- and third-generation empowerment issues, new groups continue to emerge. The gay liberation movement, which was hardly contemplated in the early struggles for civil rights, is alive and thriving in the 1990s. In a recent *New York Times* article on the Gay Games of June 1994, Stephen Holden noted:

> This proliferation of openly gay art and performance would have been unimaginable 25 years ago. Anyone who is gay or lesbian and over 40 can remember a time when the subject of homosexuality was rarely addressed by the mainstream culture. When gay characters appeared in books, plays, and movies, they were usually portrayed as tormented by their sexuality and involved in sick relationships. Or they were patronized as "decadent," to use a popular 1960s adjective expressing both disapproval and titillation.[8]

Despite the difficulties of multiculturalism, ethnicity itself is fashionable in the 1990s. The U.S. Department of Census reports a 38 percent increase in the number of citizens identifying themselves as American Indians in the last census. One theory is that individuals who formerly sought anonymity in acculturation now seek to identify with their ethnic roots and are reclaiming their Native American heritage.

Asian newscasters, black talk show hosts, movies about American Indians are common in mainstream entertainment. Public officials, athletes, and actors of all races are part and parcel of the mass media in this decade. Role models come in all colors. Music stores in cities and suburbs throughout the land carry rap alongside rock, and for good measure, a little salsa, k. d. lang, some zydaco, and the blues. Times have changed.

5

Mass Media

The Wonder Years

Network television is the prototypical Baby Boomer media, and to Boomers, television is a mirror. Television represents a friendly face, because it is their own face.

To Generation X, children of the computer and the VCR, television is not a mirror, but a window. It is another access point to the community. Network television is neither friendly nor hostile—it exists in its own sphere. Like watching your neighbors from a hiding place in a leafy tree, Xers have privately observed the proceedings for years, "eavesdropping on the adults," dropping the occasional water balloon, and drawing their own conclusions.

Boomers understand network television, and the networks understand Boomers. For them, watching television is an essentially passive, low-valued entertainment—a one-sided monologue from a friend born in the same year. It is sometimes comfortable to "watch the tube," a reflection, often superficial, of things that interest or concern us. But Generation X has a very different perspective.

To Xers, television is media, and media is the doorway to the community—a doorway that is accessible at will. Sometimes television is totally engrossing, sometimes it is wallpaper. It often reflects values, lives, and interests different from their own. For years it echoed only the speech patterns of their elders. Television often amuses. It frequently lies.

While Boomer marketers take for granted that everybody grew up with television, and that nobody doesn't watch it, we often fail to recognize that watching television is a different activity today than it was when we were young, and that not everybody views it in the same way. We are all cognizant of the technological advancements, from channel proliferation, to satellite transmission, to high definition, to interactivity, which have changed the face of The Box, but we advertisers have remained incurious about the pervasive interaction between television and our psyches, our personalities, and our world view. It is this very area we must begin to explore in order to understand the fundamental differences in the way generations view the medium and how those differences translate to the broader world of media consumption.

Media, marketing, and advertising were simpler sciences when Boomers were young. Three networks were the dominant force in television, commonly claiming to reach 95 percent or more of American households in a single night. Television viewing was a family activity, since most households owned a single set, and families commonly planned their evening around a favorite program. Adults and children were together part of massive audiences, all viewing simultaneously. For this reason, programming was most often done for the lowest common denominator, and programs that entertained both adults and children were eagerly sought and highly valued. From their earliest moments, Boomer children had a strong influence on the broadcast media, if only at first to keep it wholesome.

In retrospect, early television reflects a naíve and somehow childlike view of the world. At the forefront of the great '50s drive toward homogeneity, all television families had two amusing parents, of the same white race, who, if they slept at all, slept in twin beds. All women had the same job.

As children, we all knew Beaver's Mom. We were acquainted with Bud, Pumpkin, and Princess, as well as Aunt Bea and Uncle Miltie. Even strange old Ed Sullivan never let a Sunday night pass without "something for the kiddies." He was like a stiff, stuffy neighbor who would, nevertheless, reward us for being quiet while he visited with our parents by finally bringing out the circus or a puppet show.

Even when the stars of a show were familiar faces to our parents it didn't hurt if they also had attractive children to parade in front of the camera. Ricky Nelson ultimately became far more important to Boomers than his bandleader father, Ozzie Nelson.

Daytime television revolved around toys and schoolrooms: puppets

Kukla and Ollie, *Playschool*, and *Romper Room*. Most of the entertainment seemed designed to suit an adult's idea of something children would enjoy. The most famous puppet of all, Howdy Doody, had a life story so complex it required twin puppets to tell it completely.

> The morning sun shone a lemon-yellow over the town of Doodyville, Texas. In a small wooden shack a ranch hand named Doody smiled down at his wife who had just presented him with twin sons. The date was December 27, 1941.
>
> "Howdy," said the father to the squalling babies. At the sound of his voice they began to chortle. "That's what we'll call 'em, honey," Mr. Doody said to his wife. "Howdy will be the first one's name and since his brother is a twin we'll call him Double."[1]

Walt Disney was among the first to recognize the vast market potential represented by all those young Boomer eyeballs. With typical panache, he went straight for national television, premiering on October 27, 1954, with *Disneyland*, the first of several Walt Disney television titles. *Disneyland* promptly surpassed the popular *Arthur Godfrey and His Friends*, knocking it out of the top ten shows of the 1950s. Perhaps more notable, within the first six weeks, Disney introduced the series that made Davy Crockett more famous than most U.S. Presidents and launched a national craze for coonskin caps. With television as the springboard, Disney created or expanded the market for furry caps, Goofy lunch pails, Mickey Mouse watches, and a seemingly endless stream of merchandising goodies, which had no parallel in previous generations and thrives until this day.

The '50s also gave birth to a long line of essentially useless products bought by and for Boomers, simply because they were there to be purchased. Cheap, disposable, and utterly without redeeming social value, the list continues today, including such products as hula hoops, cereal box toys, decoder rings, candy cigarettes, "whimsy" veils, mood rings, commemorative Elvis plates, crinoline underskirts, cotton wrist bands, feminine deodorant spray, and pet rocks.

In the 1950s, magazines were mass media, too. Circulation was artificially forced to huge and unsustainable levels in an attempt to compete with network television. Magazines like *Life, Look, Collier's*, and *The Saturday Evening Post* achieved and maintained circulation bases that are unthinkable in today's more cost-conscious publishing world. The "Seven Sisters," *Good Housekeeping, Red-*

book, McCall's, Better Homes and Gardens, The Ladies' Home Journal, Woman's Day, and *Family Circle,* had a combined gross circulation of 27 million in 1955, a huge number even by today's standards. Yet, over the next ten years, as Baby Boomers left their parents' home and began to set up independent households, publishers forced circulation to a combined total of 45 million— enough to reach two out of every three women in America with tips on housekeeping, child rearing, and sex within marriage. The category peaked in 1975 at nearly 48 million and has been declining ever since. (See Figure 5–1.)

This emphasis on size and sameness throughout the '50s and early '60s helped to create the illusion of a comfortable, harmonious, and homogeneous society, in which our most urgent choices seemed to be which television program to watch or which detergent would produce the whitest laundry. Working women, blacks, or homosexuals need not apply. Indeed, to the mass media of the 1950s, such people did not exist.

Boomer childhood was sheltered and sweet. But by the end of the 1960s, a major movement had begun, one which would redefine

Figure 5–1
Total Circulation Seven Sisters 1955-1990
Circulation (millions)

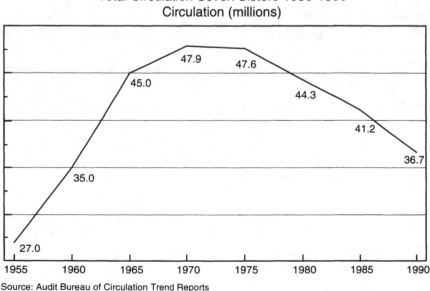

Source: Audit Bureau of Circulation Trend Reports

both Baby Boomers and the mass media and which would affect television viewing audiences for the rest of our lives and for the lives of subsequent generations. By 1968, leading-edge Boomers were twenty-five years old. This was the year that Boomer attitudes and lifestyles first began to be reflected in the mass media. It is no coincidence that 1968 marked the launch of a radical new magazine, *The Rolling Stone*. While gritty and irreverent in its early incarnation,

Rolling Stone *was the first of many media vehicles to become commercially viable by cultivating Baby Boomer sensibilities.*

The Stone was the first of many media vehicles to become commercially viable by cultivating strictly Baby Boomer sensibilities.

And 1968 was a pivotal media year in other ways. Underground newspapers and small periodicals had sprung up and thrived, as Boomer teens rejected the homogeneous 1950s pap that "commercial" media continued to offer. But it didn't stop there. Raymond Mungo, then with the alternative *Liberation News Service*, which supplied news and features to the underground press nationwide, points out that it wasn't long before *mass media* began to turn to the so-called "alternative media" for inspiration and as a source of news and entertainment. He describes the news service's move to new Washington D.C. headquarters in 1967:

> . . . The number of underground newspapers went from fifty to three hundred in a matter of a few months, and as 1968 came upon us there were suddenly *straight* newspapers, too, dailies in Pennsylvania and Iowa and California, who wanted to print our copy, dying to know where it was *at*. The mass media—UPI, the *New York Times*, CBS News—decided that we were a reliable source of information about the movement, and we had to dance around their questions. . . .[2]

The first Boomer inroads were made in the print media and in the alternative press, and they were spectacularly successful. But as Boomer power and influence grew, they simply set their sights higher. Radio was an early medium to be reinvented. FM formats, because of their superior sound, were originally the obscure haven of classical music afficionados. But when Boomers discovered how good rock and roll could sound in stereo, they literally took over the FM dial and new stations and formats blossomed overnight. The number of FM stations grew from 815 in 1960 to 2,169 in 1970 to 3,282 in 1980—an average of about fifteen stations for every market in the country. Gradually album-oriented rock became the dominant FM format, and rock and roll took over the dial from the formerly dominant old AM stations. (See Figure 5–2.)

Today, FM continues to be the dominant format in radio, accounting for 75 percent of radio audiences, according to the Radio Advertising Bureau. The story was the same for every media venue. Boomers gradually and inexorably took over, and what was first thought of as alternative media inevitably became mass media.

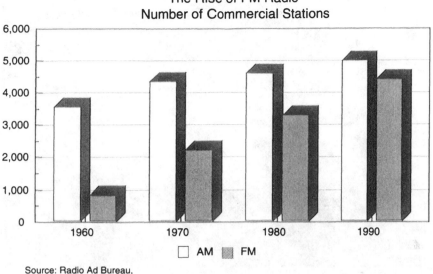

Figure 5–2
The Rise of FM Radio
Number of Commercial Stations

Source: Radio Ad Bureau,
Radio Marketing Guide and Factbook for Advertisers, 1993-1994

In many ways these new alternative papers were, like the countercul-ture that they served, the victims of their own successes. As the mass marketing of hip began in earnest in the Summer of Love, 1967, these papers' advertising revenues and circulations grew until the charm and authenticity of their underground anarchism bloated beyond recovery. At a particular point—right about the weekend of the Woodstock Fes-tival, say—so many people considered themselves members of the cul-tural underground that the term lost whatever meaning it once had.[3]

Television was slower to admit that Boomers were growing up, but daytime had made some attempt to keep up. Programs like *The Mickey Mouse Club* and *American Bandstand*, designed for "tweens" and "teens," joined the now-standard children's shows in the day-time and after-school lineup. Still, *Father Knows Best* (1954–1960), *Leave It to Beaver* (1957–1963), and *My Three Sons* (1960–1972) continued to represent the prototypical American sit-com family through the sixties.

It wasn't until January 12, 1971, with the first telecast of *All in*

Television sit-coms in the 1950s featured wholesome family groups, like the Andrews from Father Knows Best.

© 1954, 1994 CPT Holdings, courtesy Columbia Pictures Television.

the Family, that television fathers began to look less like wise old Robert Young and more like that rigid, pig-headed father we all recognize from our teenage years.

CBS introduced Archie Bunker and family as a second series entry, and it was not a hit initially. However, *All in the Family* took off during the summer reruns and then proceeded to remain among the top Nielsen-rated shows for the next nine years. It also spun off two other successful series, *Maude* and *The Jeffersons*. Part of this success was due to Archie's ability to break down the artificial barriers of convention that had held back television during the 1950s. For the first time, characters on television were talking and acting the way that people really talked and acted.

The show explored the generational conflict of the early 1970s and discussed mature themes in frank language. Even though Archie used racial epithets like "jungle-bunnies," the show was popular with black audiences too. It was one of the first to use black actors as ongoing characters and to portray those characters

By the early 1970s, television fathers looked less like the wise Robert Young and more like the pigheaded Archie Bunker.

All in the Family © 1971, 1994 ELP Communications, courtesy Columbia Pictures Television.

as smarter and more sophisticated than the (white) leading man. *All in the Family* clearly represented the politically correct point of view for the times. Archie himself was the butt of the joke as, again and again, his prejudices were held up for ridicule.

Archie's daughter, Gloria, and her husband, Micheal (Meathead) Stivic, clearly represented the Boomer point of view. They were eloquent in professing all the "ideologically correct" positions of the day on civil rights, the war in Vietnam, sexual freedom, and tolerance. Moreover, the Boomer point of view was also validated by Archie's wife, Edith, the neighbors, and occasional guests. Gradually, issue by issue, episode by episode, even Archie was converted.

Archie may engage in argument after argument, but when the shouting has died down, he's the one who inevitably changes. Inch by inch, issue by issue, when the crunch comes, he learns to see things from a different point of view, especially when things move from vague generalities to specific people. For instance, he may subscribe to the general rhetoric of some neighborhood Ku Klux Klan members, but when they earmark Michael and Gloria's house for a burning cross, Archie is a thundering bull, proudly citing the black blood in his veins (from a transfusion during a gall bladder operation) and threatening to call on his "black blood brothers" to help him stomp on any "honkies" who want to mess with him.[4]

With *All in the Family*, Producer Normal Lear had accomplished the most significant foray into Boomer lifestyles and values made by television since Walt Disney. And television was forever changed as a result.

And as newly adult Boomers captured first the alternative and then the mainstream media, they began for the first time to understand that they had the power to change the world. As Boomers embraced political action and civil rights, the first strong black characters began to appear on network television. Before he was Dr. Cliff Huxtable, Bill Cosby was the first African-American man to play a leading role in a regular prime-time series. This breakthrough was especially important at the time because the role was dramatic and the character he portrayed might easily have been played by a white actor. Cosby was teamed with Robert Culp in *I Spy*. The plot held that he was a U.S. government agent, working undercover as a manager/companion to Culp's role (also a spy) as philandering tennis bum. Prior to this time, most black roles on television or in the movies were comic stereotypes, servants, or drug dealers. As hard as it may seem to believe now, *I Spy* made history in 1965.

In a very short time, middle-class blacks became *de rigueur* as part of each network's programming schedule. *Julia* (1968), *The Mod Squad* (1968), *The Flip Wilson Show* (1970), and *The Jeffersons* (1975) were among the stronger television entries that featured black actors as leads or principal characters in prime time.

In television news, Boomers played a more aggressive role, becoming ever more attuned to the niceties of media manipulation as they gained experience. From the Summer of Love in 1967 to the Clinton inauguration in 1993, the media life of Boomers has been bound up in Be-ins, Love-ins, Happenings, Hootenannies, Marches, Demonstrations, Picket Lines, Live-Aid, Farm-Aid, AIDS awareness, and one extravagent and newsworthy media event after another:

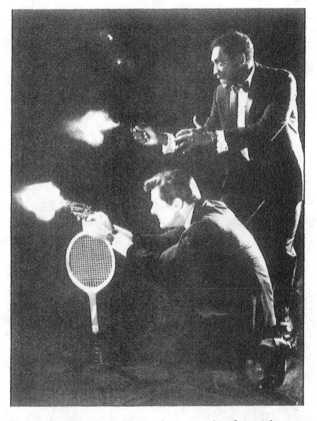

In I Spy *(1965), Bill Cosby was the first African-American man to play a leading role in a regular prime-time series.*

Courtesy of Three F Productions.

Within two hours I was on the steps of San Francisco City Hall in front of four television cameras, five photographers, four newspaper reporters, and seven radio stations, denouncing HUAC* as a "witch hunter." . . . I raved, "The government is trying to stifle anti-war dissent."

The press hung on every word. I was playing Angry Radical, but inside I was laughing, standing on my hands and turning somersaults.

---

*House Un-American Activities Committee.

HUAC was not stifling dissent, but stimulating it—to greater and greater heights.

—Jerry Rubin in *Do It!* on being subpoenaed by the House Un-American Activities Committee[5]

The techniques of media manipulation, learned by Boomers in the 1960s, were never forgotten. In fact, these techniques are part and parcel of the Baby Boomer's basic way of relating to media, and as we shall see, this is a pattern to which they return time and time again.

During the 1970s, things were deceptively quiet. Boomers, leading edge now in their thirties, withdrew a little from public life to concentrate on the private and personal. By now, mass media was firmly in their pocket, as advertisers had discovered the wisdom of supporting media targeted to Baby Boomers. The market for goods and services expanded, slowly at first, and then more rapidly, as Boomers got married, got jobs, had kids, and then got divorced.

Television reflected the Boomer predeliction for divorce, and helped to redefine our view of the basic family unit. A series of new shows debuted, featuring less traditional households. In *The Courtship of Eddie's Father* (1969–1972), a widower raises his son alone, and seems content not to remarry, even though his son, played by Brandon Cruz, is constantly searching for a suitable second mother. In *The Odd Couple* (1970–1975), two divorced men set up housekeeping and proceed to bicker like an old married couple.

One of the most radical shows of the 1970s was *One Day at a Time* (1975–1984) in which a modern young divorcée struggled to raise two teenage daughters. This was not only the first significant network acknowledgment of divorce, but the first time a divorced woman (played by Bonnie Franklin) was shown as heroine.

Even *Laverne and Shirley* (1976–1983) were metamorphosed. When first introduced as minor characters on *Happy Days*, our girls were rather disreputable "bimbos." By 1976 they had become honest, young, single, blue-collar women—not June Cleaver, but still "good girls," despite the fact that they had no husbands.

Finally, in *Three's Company* (1977–1984), two young women lived with a single male roommate. To gain the landlord's approval, the male roomie, played by John Ritter, posed as a homosexual—thus, in theory, eliminating any chance of hanky-panky with the girls. Suddenly, we

Shows like The Courtship of Eddie's Father *were representative of the "nontraditional" family as viewed on early 1970s television.*

were talking about unmarried parents, same-sex roommates, mixed-sex roommates, homosexuality, and D-I-V-O-R-C-E. Sex was still implied, rather than graphic, with pages of coy dialogue and titillating situations. Prime-time television had traveled far from the days of the twin bed.

Magazines remained slightly ahead of the curve. *Ms* was launched in 1972, introducing Boomers and the world to the principles of feminism. Magazines like *Black Enterprise* (1970) and *Hispanic Business* (1979) were launched to service newly acknowledged middle-class minorities. *Look, Life,* and *The Saturday Evening Post* had significantly downsized or collapsed altogether under the weight of their giant circulations. There began a proliferation of smaller, more selective magazine titles.

Ms. Magazine, launched in 1972, introduced Boomers to the principles of feminism.

© Reprinted by permission of *Ms.* Magazine.

Boomers used the 1970s as the time to redefine themselves. It was as if they awoke one fine morning and realized, *en masse*, that they could not dance in the park forever. During the 1970s, individual career opportunities began to arrive—suddenly there was

Magazines like Black Enterprise *(1970) were launched in the 1970s to service newly acknowledged, middle-class ethnic markets.*

© Copyright *Black Enterprise* Magazine, August 1970. Earl G. Graves Publishing Co., New York, NY.

room at the top, as the Silent and GI Generations aged and retired. One by one, the Woodstock Generation went to work.

Sometime during this decade, Boomers traded in the old Volkswagen for a Toyota, cut their hair, checked into the Betty Ford clinic, became stockbrokers, and emerged again in the '80s as . . .

Yuppies.

Young, upwardly mobile, professional people replaced the radical hipsters of the '60s. Now approaching forty, our new heroes were the Carringtons and J. R. Ewing and that ultimate '80s Boomer Gordon Gekko. Flower power was out. Civil causes stood aside. Greed and money were "in," as Boomers rushed to seize and conquer all that they had ignored and ridiculed in their youth. As Winston Churchill once observed, "If you were not a liberal when you were twenty, you have no heart. But if you have not become a conservative by the time you are forty, you have no brains."

Boomers became conservative enough to elect Ronald Reagan to the Presidency. Then they embarked on a decade-long orgy of self-indulgence and conspicuous consumption. Shopping took on the status of an Olympic sport, as recently affluent Boomers set out upon a spending spree that had not been matched since the 1920s. Those marketers who had successfully targeted Boomers earlier now reaped obscene rewards, as Boomers drove up sales of BMWs, leisure clothing, business suits, electronic equipment, jewelry, furs, and vacation time shares.

Working women were an especially good market, as they armed themselves for business success with clothes, credit cards, assertiveness training, automobiles, and his-and-her Rolexes. Women, who had comprised less than 25 percent of new car buyers in 1970, became over one-third the market by 1980 and now represent nearly half of all automobile sales. (See Figure 5–3.)

Clothing manufacturers and designers like Donna Karan, Ann Klein, and Escada became household words and John T. Molloy's *Dress for Success* was the bible for fashion in the 1980s.

The television sit-com remained standard viewing fare, but we were also introduced to that hallmark of '80s enlightenment the "prime-time soap." As Boomers struggled with careers and business, our media heroes also aspired to power and riches. We were fascinated with J. R. Ewing, a man who never let ethics stand in the

Figure 5–3
Women as Percent of New Car Buyers
1970-1990

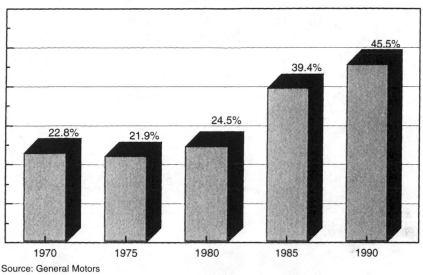

Source: General Motors

way of personal aggrandizement. And with Gordon Gekko, the character from *Wall Street* who uttered that ultimate Yuppie maxim, "Greed is good. Greed works."

And suddenly the actors were older. Alan Alda, Linda Evans, and Joan Collins dominated the small screen, some well past their fiftieth birthday. These actors were admired as much for retaining their youthful appearance as for their talent and ability.

Elizabeth Taylor remained our most celebrated movie star, even though it was twenty years since she had made a film. Lauren Hutton and Cheryl Teigs were representative of the newly idealized forty-year-old cover girl. To paraphrase a popular commercial, Boomers were not getting older; they were getting better.

When *TV Guide* picked the top television shows of the 1980s, the casts were studded with forty- and fifty-year-old actors. From the aging cast of *Dallas* to the balding proprietor of *Cheers*, network television did not lack for Baby Boomer role models. One show, *The Wonder Years*, was made whole-cloth from Boomer nostalgia. But Generation X was represented only by the Cosby kids. (See Figure 5–4.)

Figure 5–4
TV Guide Picks the Top
Television Shows of the 1980s

1. The Cosby Show	8. Miami Vice
2. Dallas	9. Wheel of Fortune
3. Hill Street Blues	10. LA Law
4. Dynasty	11. Sat Night Live
5. Nightline	12. Golden Girls
6. Cheers	13. Tabloid TV
7. Moonlighting	14. Wonder Years
	15. St Elsewhere

Source: The TV Guide TV Book 1992
Note: mini-series and specials omitted

We had the very old (Miss Ellie, Dr. Eldridge, *The Golden Girls*), and we had the very young (John Ross Ewing, Vanessa Cosby), but there were few examples of the generation in between. Except on *Saturday Night Live*, the face of the twenty-year-old was conspicuously missing from network television. As Liz Murphy, age twenty-four, put it, "They went straight from *thirtysomething* to *90210*. They skipped me completely."

Popular nighttime shows in the 1980s also traded in the kind of glitz and glamour that reinforced the Boomer/Yuppie's newfound lust for affluence and position. Yuppie families of all colors sought to emulate the Cosby family: doctor-father, lawyer-mother, articulate and always well-dressed children. Yuppie professionals privately measured their real-life offices against the decorator furniture and designer clothing seen in the offices of *LA Law*. Cybil Shepherd wrote the book on dressing for success in *Moonlighting*, even though her struggling detective agency never betrayed any visible means of support.

And working women were everywhere. Gone was the self-effacing mother who had waited patiently for Lassie to come home. Gone, too, was the ditsy redhead who couldn't do anything right. In their places we found tough, divorced, expensively dressed women, who were "at home in the boardroom, as well as the bedroom."

And what of Boomer causes? Boomer demonstrations? Nobody much was marching on Reagan's Washington. Instead, Boomers had discovered a new kind of social statement: *Live Aid*. Spearheaded by Boomer Bob Geldoff and the English bands who first staged *Band Aid*, a star-studded concert in support of relief for Bangladesh, *Live Aid* was the first American "charity" extravaganza. Televised on ABC on Saturday, July 13, 1985, *Live Aid* delivered a twelve household rating and, more important, was heavily watched by the all-important 18–49 age group. Advertisers got their money's worth, America leapt upon the "Aid" bandwagon with typical Baby Boomer energy, and other charity concerts soon followed.

It was the perfect way to support a good cause, raise significant sums of money, entertain themselves, and celebrate generational solidarity all at the same time. Boomers could be socially responsible without distracting themselves from the pursuit of the '80s good life.

But at last, the decade crashed to a close, and we now find our Boomers in the grip of a predictable 1990s midlife crisis, wallowing in nostalgia, and trying to stay young. And the mass media is still hard on their heels with loads of diet and exercise advice, fashion for the over-forty crowd, and reunion after reunion of sit-coms made popular long ago.

Unfortunately, the Baby Boom has maxed out. It will never grow larger than it was in 1970. In 1980, the total population of Generation X surpassed the Boom. And, coincidently, in 1980 network television ratings began to decline. As long as Boomers grew, in numbers and in influence, network television thrived. ABC, NBC, and CBS dominated the television landscape. They captured between them more than 90 percent of all the sets in use in 1960 and 1970. (The balance of televisions were tuned to independent stations, public TV, or cable.) Today that same number is closer to 50 percent.

This well-documented decline in network ratings has been popularly attributed to the proliferation of cable programming, VCRs, and other such viewing alternatives, and these improvements in television technology have contributed to changing viewing patterns. But cable and VCRs were available before 1980, so the existence of the technology did not change habits all by itself. As discussed in subsequent chapters, the difference in 1980 was that the new technology found a market among those people who had ceased to find network television compelling. Cable, VCRs, and the like filled the vacuum that was created by the networks themselves. Throughout the 1980s, the content of most network programming, with Boomer characters and middle-aged adult issues, had very little of interest to Generation X. (See Figure 5–5.)

And magazines did not do a better job of appealing to Xers. The editorial content of most major magazines remained tied to Boomers, and publishers courted them in the same way that network television did.

We can calculate a "rating" for magazines, by dividing total newsstand sales by total U.S. population (adults 18 +). This tells us, for example, that in 1960 there were fifty-one copies of ABC-measured magazines sold on the newsstand for every one hundred adults living in the United States. We used only newsstand sales in this analysis, since subscription sales, which can be manipulated

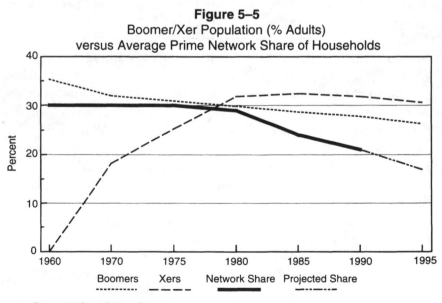

Figure 5–5
Boomer/Xer Population (% Adults)
versus Average Prime Network Share of Households

Boomers   Xers   Network Share   Projected Share

Source: McCann-Erikson Research
Statistical Abstract of the U.S. 1991

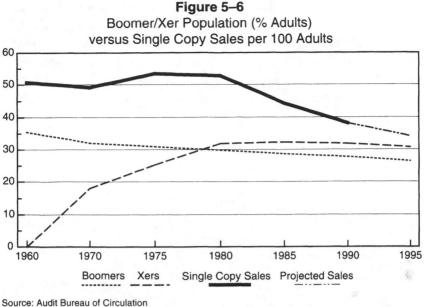

Figure 5–6
Boomer/Xer Population (% Adults)
versus Single Copy Sales per 100 Adults

Boomers   Xers   Single Copy Sales   Projected Sales

Source: Audit Bureau of Circulation
Statistical Abtract of the U.S. 1991

with special offers, premiums, and long-term renewals, are much slower to respond to demographic changes. (See Figure 5–6.)

Like network television ratings, newsstand sales of magazines have been in gradual decline since 1980—the same year that Generation X gained the majority in population. As with television, we have seen a proliferation of smaller, more selective magazine titles, which gained circulation at the expense of larger, more established magazines. But the audience pie did not get substantially bigger. As Generation X failed to adopt *The Ladies' Home Journal* or *Time*, these magazines were required by the economics of the marketplace to reduce their rate base and to compete for both readers and advertising revenue with upstart titles like *Working Woman, Shape*, and *Details*.

In the early 1980s Generation X began to take control of the television set. Their influence was slight at first. But throughout the 1980s, their adult numbers grew. And as they increased their expendable income, as they took over the shopping malls and the remote controls, their influence grew. The effect has not been revolutionary, as it was with Boomers. Rather, it has been evolutionary. Boomers pounced upon the media, like Jack Nicholson announcing "Heeeeere's Johnny!" Xers in the '80s made slow and subtle inroads, working first into those dayparts that Boomers had largely vacated: daytime, late night, and syndication. But, as we shall see, their effect on the media has been no less profound.

6

Growing Up X

Rumor, Scandal, and Trash TV

Boomers still tend to think of watching television as something that families do together in the living room. They want television to be a "safe" place for the children and often assume it is—even when it isn't. Boomer marketers tend to think of television, especially network television, as something that "everybody" does and, therefore, something that we all have in common.

However, television viewing for Generation X children was a significantly different experience than it was for Boomer children. To begin with, Xers have never known a world without a television in every household. While some younger Boomers also knew television from an early age, Boomer children saw a much different version of the "boob tube." Much of early television programming was simply boring and badly produced. As a consequence, early television was much less compelling than it is today. It was black and white. The local station went off the air late at night. Most children were not encouraged to spend too many hours watching, for fear it would "ruin their eyes" or rob them of sunshine. Many families could not afford television sets, and many that could found the viewing limited by poor over-the-air reception, weak antennae, or aging picture tubes. Television was neither portable nor pervasive. Only one channel could be viewed at a time, and there was no way to recover programming that ran at an inconvenient time.

It was a vastly different medium than the ubiquitous, intrusive television of Generation X's childhood. By the time Generation X started to watch, television sets and television programming had evolved to new levels of sophistication. The technology was better and cheaper. Production techniques and audience research were vastly improved. Not only did everybody have a set, but most households had more than one. Weary working parents often gave up any attempt to moderate viewing by children. Boomers noted that television never hurt *them*, and in fact, many children were encouraged to watch television by parents or teachers who believed that certain programs were educational. In truth, television was often a safer alternative for latchkey kids than playing in the streets unattended.

As latchkey children in single-parent households, Xers spent more time alone with the tube than Boomers did. And with less benefit of adult family around after school and at night, Xers often turned to the media as a way to learn about the world. The static, school-like *Romper Room* was quickly replaced by action heroes and color cartoons, produced for children—not for parents. Many Xers learned to read and count with Big Bird, and later they learned about romance and prostitution, homosexuality, violence, music, guns, and money from prime-time movies, the soaps, talk shows, and the news.

Xers were used to watching television alone or with their young friends. They seldom watched with their families. The proliferation of multiset households that took place in the '60s and '70s meant that for Xers, television viewing had evolved into a solitary and highly individualized activity, while they were still very young children. (See Figure 6–1.)

Families no longer gathered around the television set, with TV trays and Uncle Miltie. First came transistorized "portables," which were dragged from room to room to keep Generation X amused while doing the dishes or doing their homework or even while visiting with friends. Later came battery-operated sets, some small enough to be carried in a pocket. Television could, and did, go anywhere: to the street corner, to work, camping, school. For many Xers, television was their babysitter, their entertainment, their teacher, and their night-light.

Networks were not required to program for family viewing (wholesomeness) because in fact, families did not view television together. Network programmers, as we shall see, were not only aware of this fact but exploited it, as did advertisers who sought to market products to this newly isolated target market. As media technology

Figure 6-1
Growth of Multi-Set Households

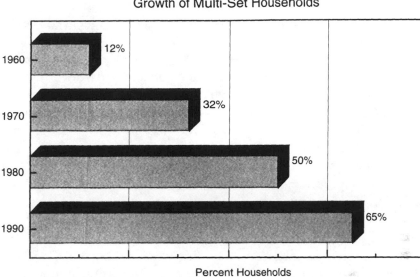

Percent Households

Source: McCann-Erickson Research
A.C. Nielsen

and the "science" of marketing began to converge in the mid-1960s, our Xers were very young children. And, as very young children, they became the object of a media feeding frenzy in which the networks exploited and abused their willingness to believe and fed their curiosity with bizarre plot lines, monster characters, and heroes designed not to inspire values, but to sell toys. Advertisers, likewise, helped create for many children a dissatisfaction with their basic circumstances as they pitched toys, games, and candy to rich and poor alike, suggesting that friends would admire you, your family would be happy, your grades would improve, and your teeth would never have cavities if only your parents would buy Brand X.

The situation was so blatantly callous, it eventually attracted the attention of watchdog groups such as the Action for Children's Television. In response to such pressure groups, the Federal Communications Commission (FCC) issued stringent guidelines for children's programming in 1974, but by then many of our Xers had already developed a healthy skepticism about advertising and a love/hate relationship with the media.

In order to understand how this came to be, it is necessary to briefly review some of the history of network television and to discuss some of the behind-the-scenes concepts that influenced the development of the industry.

A series of events took place during the late 1950s and early 1960s that set the stage for the changing face of network programming. The first, and most dramatic, of these was the shift in power over programming from the sponsor to the network. Prior to the mid-1960s, most network shows were "sponsored," that is, controlled by advertisers who paid for both the costs to produce the program and the network time. More powerful sponsors had first crack at the premium prime-time slots. All had a great deal of control over the content of the programming they sponsored.

This changed abruptly in 1959, a result of the infamous "quiz show scandals." One of the most popular program formats of 1958 was the big-money quiz show. The first was *The $64,000 Question*. As the name describes, contestants answered very difficult questions on a preselected topic, and the grand prize was $64,000. Since the contestants were required to accomplish this feat over the course of several weekly appearances, many of them became quite well known to the viewing public, and some retained a measure of celebrity long after the show had been canceled. Among the early contenders, for example, was Dr. Joyce Brothers, who won $64,000 by answering a series of questions on the subject of boxing. Dr. Brothers, a psychologist, later published books and became a popular television/radio personality, enjoying a long career in that role.

Then, as now, popular programming invites imitation. Soon there were several such shows, including *Twenty-One, The $64,000 Challenge*, and *Tic, Tac, Dough*. The prime-time quiz show format blossomed. New shows were launched, with nervous contestants and larger and larger prizes—until it was revealed that some of the contestants had been supplied with the answers in advance.

Months of rumors, fanned by several magazine articles and fueled by accusations of mal-practice by a former contestant on *Twenty-One*, Herbert Stempel, led to an investigation early in 1959 by a New York grand jury. The probe of quiz show "rigging" was pursued further in the House of Representatives that fall by the Special Subcommittee on Legislative Oversight, headed by Rep. Oren Harris. On Nov 2 came the

confession from the key witness, Charles Van Doren, who had previously denied having any knowledge of cheating on *Twenty-One*, the program on which he became a national celebrity after defeating Stempel.[1]

The prime time quiz show came crashing down, as audiences re-
acted with outrage. Two other popular quiz shows, *The $64,000
Question* and *The $64,000 Challenge*, were also implicated by wit-
nesses. Although top network executives denied any knowledge of
wrongdoing, several of the producers were banned from the industry, and sponsors (most notably Revlon) were roundly criticized for
the role they played in encouraging producers to eliminate unat-
tractive contestants. The integrity of the entire commercial broadcasting industry was brought into question and ultimately subjected
to increased regulation by the government. Honest sponsors hur-
ried to put as much distance as possible between themselves and
the improprieties, and the public's fascination with big-money quiz
shows dissipated overnight.

At about the same time, network executives devised a new way
to sell advertising, one which not only protected sponsors in the
face of such a scandal but also happened to result in enormous
profit to the networks. This new invention was called "the scatter
plan." Under a scatter plan, an advertiser could buy spots of commercial time in a variety of programs without taking any responsibility at all for the content of the shows. Production costs (which
had escalated under the old system) were borne by the network or
by independent producers. The scatter advertiser simply participat-
ed by paying for the time that he used. This plan allowed an individual advertiser to spend less because he was paying only for a few
minutes of time rather than for the entire program. At the same
time, it allowed the network to charge more for each single minute
of time because the cost was spread among a larger base of advertisers. It involved less risk to the advertiser because he could spread
his investment over a larger number of programs rather than
putting all his dollars into one or two shows, which might or might
not be a hit with the viewing public. Scatter sales were not only a
boon to the large advertiser but also allowed advertisers with smaller budgets to venture into television. Suddenly the potential market
for commercial time was vastly enlarged.

And as for the viewing public, they saw improved programming, less blatant commercialism, and programming that was presumed free of corrupt influences. The price to viewers was a continuing increase in the number and length of commercial interruptions. But as the entertainment value of television programming continued to improve, viewers seemed to accept the increasing number of commercials with little more than the occasional grumble.

Gradually, the concept of sponsoring whole programs lost popularity, as production costs continued to escalate beyond the means of most advertisers. The concept of sponsorship was replaced by the concept of buying audiences, sometimes even having the network guarantee that the scatter plan or schedule an advertiser bought would deliver a predetermined number of households or viewers. If it failed to do so, the network would simply add spots to the original schedule, at no cost, until the desired number of rating points had been achieved.

According to Gordon Link, who was then Vice President of Sales at ABC, "The scatter plan was the mechanism which ushered in the true golden age of television, and the mechanism which finally gave programming control to the networks." At last, the networks could decide what to air without interference from the sponsors, and the changes soon became apparent. Gone were the commercial plugs that used to interject themselves at odd moments into every script. Characters in a show used products that suited the story line, not the sponsor, and sometimes these characters even made fun of advertised products if they wished. The best prime-time slots were allocated to the most popular programming (as measured by Nielsen ratings) and not necessarily to the sponsor with the largest pocketbook. Gradually, the networks gained strength and independence from sponsors, whose play-it-safe value systems were largely seen to inhibit creativity and experimentation.

As the value of each rating point increased, the networks became less afraid of offending some viewers than they were of losing the audience ratings wars. Network programmers grew bolder as the '50s gave way to the '60s. Liberal (Boomer) social values had increasing influence, and once-taboo subjects like sex, race relations, and drugs were openly referenced in prime time.

The twin bed was permanently consigned to the television attic, and sexual innuendo, titillation, and mature themes were now the stuff of successful sit-coms. With only three networks available until 1990, the demand for advertising time was invariably higher than the amount of time available. The networks carefully gauged public reaction by measuring the number of eyeballs in front of the set, and they never went so far that they could not retreat in the face of falling ratings. As their wealth and power grew, so did the level of sophistication they brought to the new "science" of programming (translation: the new "science" of delivering audiences to advertisers). This science was based on two principles: the principle of audience availability and the principle of audience flow.

The principle of audience availability held that it was easier, for example, to attract men to the set in the evenings since a normal daytime work schedule meant that most men were not at home during the day and, hence, not "available" to join daytime audiences. Daytime television, therefore, should be programmed for women viewers, who were presumed to be available.

In order to draw the largest number of male viewers, in order to maximize the available audience, a male-oriented program should be scheduled at night, when more men were at home. It was this reasoning that led ABC, in 1970, to convince the National Football League to play some of their games at night so they could be broadcast in prime time. *Monday Night Football* has ever since delivered the largest consistently male viewing audience in television, and football has become America's most profitable franchise sport.

The principle of audience flow holds that it is easier to maintain and build upon an existing audience than to attract one in the first place. Therefore, once you have successfully attracted a following among a desirable audience, you should do your best to keep them watching. Once ABC had men watching football, they would not schedule a cooking show to follow the game because few women are in the audience, and the men who tuned in for the football are not likely to stay tuned in for the cooking. Instead, ABC scheduled news or detective shows, which were more likely to encourage men to stay in their recliners and keep their hands off the channel knob.

Techniques of counterprogramming, based on audience availability and audience flow, acted to further divide and isolate segments of the viewing public. Since ABC's *Monday Night Football* had a dominant and unshakable hold on male viewers, CBS countered with programs designed to appeal to women viewers. This was also based on the concept of audience availability. For if all the

In 1970, ABC convinced the National Football League to play some of their games at night, in order to be broadcast in prime time, and draw the largest number of male viewers.

Monday Night Football, ABC Photography Department © 1990 Copyright Capital Cities/ABC, Inc. courtesy ABC-TV.

men were watching football, that left a great untapped audience of women viewers without entertainment. After some experimenting, CBS hit the jackpot in 1974 with a lineup of their strongest half-hour sit-coms. They started at 8:00 P.M. with *Rhoda*, followed by *Phyllis, All in the Family*, and *Maude*, running until 10:00 P.M. CBS finished off the night with the one-hour drama *Medical Center*. According to A. C. Nielsen, all of these programs finished the 1974 season ranking in the top ten.

The first of Generation X were born after the quiz show scandals and after the birth of the scatter plan. In their most formative years, broadcasters were taking irrevocable steps toward the reckless pursuit of ratings and moving toward more controversial programming standards. Xers missed all those corny, wholesome shows created by sponsors for family viewing. They never saw the *Texaco Star Theater* or *Your Show of Shows* or *The Ed Wynn Show*. Instead, they watched television according to the rules of audience availability and audience flow.

Except for the morning cartoon, programs that appealed to women were scheduled during the day, when women were presumed to be at home alone. Children's shows dominated Saturday morning. Monday night was for men, and Saturday night was for adolescents and others without dates.

Viewers were forced to choose between their two or three most favorite shows of the week, which inevitably appeared on the networks directly opposite one another. Over time, the networks actually trained audiences to expect to see certain types of programming at certain times. Habit worked in their favor, as audiences tuned in for favorite programs and stayed to see new ones.

Network schedules purposely divided the larger viewing audience into smaller, more homogeneous groups of viewers. This had two effects: It allowed advertisers to identify children as a cost-efficient target market in selected dayparts, and it accelerated the trend to racier dialogue and more controversial subject matter in dayparts where Generation X was not supposed to be part of the audience.

A side effect of splitting larger audiences into subgroups is the effect the more homogeneous audiences have on the programming. If the audience is largely women, for example, the cast of *Designing Women* can make jokes about workmen who wear their pants slung too low without fear of offending the average man, who is not watching. If women were watching sexy sit-coms, that left the door open for the men in the audience to be given larger doses of so-called male-oriented programming: sports, Arnold Schwarzenegger, *Miami Vice*. The children were supposed to be in bed or watching innocent cartoons. So by the time the mid-1980s rolled around, bullets flew, blood was shed in abundance, and light profanity had become acceptable. Sexuality was increasingly treated in an adult manner. Splitting the audience into male and female groups and by age groups turned out to be the first step toward separating audiences according to their tolerance for graphic violence, foul language, sexually explicit material, and racial humor.

Part of the rationale for allowing greater latitude in language and subject matter on television is that the audience is expected to exhibit a specific composition based on its time position in the network lineup. Traditionally, the emphasis remained on programming suitable for families early in the evening, with more controversial programming scheduled later, when the kids were presumed to be in bed. Part of the rationale used by CBS in designing their "blockbuster" sit-com night opposite *Monday Night Football* was that they wanted to move the controversial *All in the Family* and *Maude* to the 9:00 P.M. time slot, outside the "family viewing hours."

We have already noted the dependence on television that many Generation X children exhibited. And while the networks frequently answered complaints about sex and violence with the assurance that these shows were aired outside "family viewing hours," the only catch was that *the children were not always watching what and when they were supposed to be watching.* The fact is that children were often viewing television at 9:00 P.M. or later. Working parents and single parents found it difficult to closely monitor their children's viewing. Children watched television around the clock and not always at home. And the fact that families no longer watched television together exacerbated the problem for everyone.

By 1970, it became necessary for the average household to have access to more than one television set, since Mom could hardly watch her movie while Dad was watching sports, unless she had her own set. Luckily, young Boomer parents were into spending money on television sets.

While they were at it, the television might as well be color. Most of Generation X has never watched television in black and white. When the first Xers were born in 1961, American television was black and white. But color set usage grew quickly, fueled by millions of younger Boomer families, all setting up house and buying furniture. Thus, by the time the leading edge of Generation X was ten years old, four out of ten households had color television. They were not only free to view sex and violence as children but were also allowed to view their sex and violence "in living color"—a phrase that would later be resurrected by Fox TV in a different context for their notorious Saturday night comedy show. (See Figure 6–2.)

Television commercials for children were rare in the 1950s and early 1960s, when sponsorship was the rule. Most advertisers considered television too expensive for children's products. But by the late 1960s those same factors that tended to divide and isolate television audiences in other dayparts also provided a relatively "pure"

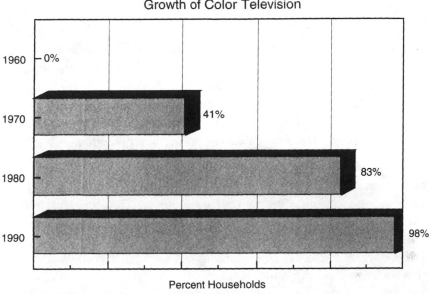

Figure 6–2
Growth of Color Television

1960 0%

1970 41%

1980 83%

1990 98%

Percent Households

Source: McCann-Erickson Research
        A.C. Nielsen

audience of children on Saturday mornings. Since advertisers had been relieved of sponsorship costs, and audiences were no longer inflated with adult viewers, some advertisers took the opportunity to advertise their products directly to children.

The networks encouraged them with expanded programming, mostly cartoons airing on Saturday morning. These shows utilized a new, limited animation technique, involving fewer movements per second, which allowed the networks to produce cartoon shows in quantity and relatively inexpensively. Commercial time was expanded within each program to nearly twice what it was in prime time. Saturday morning shows carried as many as sixteen minutes of advertising time per hour, as compared to the 9.5 minutes per hour permitted in prime time under the Television Code. Finally, children's preference for the familiar allowed each program to be rerun up to six times, meaning that fewer episodes needed to be produced.

The "kids" daypart quickly became a huge profit center for the networks, with commercial pricing ranging as high as $22,000 per minute depending on the ratings and the time of year. By 1974,

Saturday daytime was an $80 million business for the three networks, growing to more than $250 million by the late 1980s.

> Citizens groups did not become aroused, however, until the networks began to deal excessively—in their competitive zeal—with monsters, grotesque superheroes and gratuitous violence to win the attention of youngsters. Advertisers, by then, were making the most of the gullibility of children by pitching sugar-coated cereals, candy-coated vitamins, and expensive toys (some retailing for as much as $50) in shrewdly made commercials that often verged on outright deception.[3]

Broadcast reformers objected to the overcommercialization of children's television, arguing with some justification that targeting sophisticated commercials to undiscriminating children was unfair marketing practice. A great many of the popular programs were built around dolls or other toys: *Strawberry Shortcake, The Smurfs, My Little Pony*, and later the *Teenage Mutant Ninja Turtles*. Not only did they carry advertising, but the shows themselves were virtual commercials. In other cases, brand names were actively promoted by program hosts, often characterized as teachers, sheriffs, or firemen, but who in reality acted as salespeople for toys, cereal, and the like.

In 1974, the FCC issued the Children's Television Policy Statement, offering guidelines for children's programming. The report, issued in response to petitions from consumer groups like Action for Children's Television, emphasized that because children are immature and have special needs, broadcasters are obligated to provide a reasonable amount of programming for them, and that a large part of that programming should be educational. But it was not until 1990 that the Children's Television Act, which imposes limits on the commercialization of kid's television, came into effect. By that time, the youngest of Generation X was nine years old and no longer as gullible as he used to be.

Generation X understands very well that watching television involves watching commercials. Many of Generation X learned the hard way, and at an early age, that the cereal that sounds so healthy may not be good for your teeth, that a new game does not guarantee that your family will gather around you in a happy, loving circle, that often the toy you want most is too expensive for your mother to buy or much smaller than it looked on television. They learned, in short, that television tells "lies." This was a hard lesson. But it was learned by many children and passed down from them to other children, to friends and siblings, as children talked together about what they saw on Saturday mornings while their working parents slept late or ran errands or watched the news in the next room.

This was another event in the series of life experiences for Xers which contributed to their well-deserved reputation as skeptics and scoffers and accounts in part for their strong aversion to "hype," particularly in advertising. It may be that advertisers in the 1990s will have to pay now for the abuses of the industry in the '60s, '70s, and '80s. We made skeptics of Generation X before they entered grade school, and since then we have done little to convince them that we can be trusted after all.

By the time Generation X was ten, familiar sit-com families were breaking up into those "nontraditional" families that better reflected the new Boomer lifestyle: single parents, "blended families," and people simply living together. But the already cynical Xer was not impressed with television's new relevance:

> The Brady Bunch, The Partridge Family, The Courtship of Eddie's Father, and Nanny and the Professor all concerned widows and widowers, not divorcés. Talk about denial.
> —Jeff Giles, "Generalizations X," Newsweek

Boomers found these programs ground-breaking and risqué compared to earlier sit-coms. Generation X, whose real-life families were in the midst of divorces, separations, and the stress of dual careers in high gear, found them amusing fantasies. However, they did get the jokes. Prime time programs like *Maude* (1972), *One Day at a Time* (1975), *Sanford and Son* (1971), and *Barney Miller* (1975) also dealt humorously with sex, drugs, and scandal—and by age ten, most Xers could appreciate the humor.

After all, they had been watching *Donahue* (1967). Despite the fact that the frank talk show aired outside the "family viewing hours" when kids were expected to be at school, kids were watching *Donahue*. After school, in the summertime, and on school holidays, they watched Phil and various guests discuss wife abuse, heroin addiction, homosexuality, violence in the schools, transvestitism, and similar topics, which often held their interest more than the fifth rerun of *Simba the White Lion*.

*Luke and Laura (Genie Francis and Anthony Geary),
whose steamy romance inspired the plot of* General
Hospital *kept Generation X glued to their televisions
in the afternoon.*

© 1993 Copyright Capital Cities/ABC, Inc. Courtesy ABC-TV.

And everything they heard about on *Donahue,* they saw dramatically portrayed on *General Hospital* (1963), *The Young and the Restless* (1973), or *Ryan's Hope* (1975). As Generation X entered their teen years and throughout their twenties, the daytime soaps were perhaps the only genre that consistently featured young characters dealing with many of the same trials and tribulations that Xers themselves recognized and felt strongly about—romance, dangerous behavior, career choices, family strife, and sex.

Originally written for housewives, daytime dramas were an enduring tradition in the American media. First popular on the radio, some "soaps" date as far back as half a century. But the face of the soap opera audience changed in the mid-1970s as *General Hospital* became the first daytime drama to successfully capture a large number of young, teenage viewers. By the late 1970s, the plot lines of *General Hospital* were reported in local newspapers, and fan clubs had sprung up around the country. The cast featured rock star Rick Springfield, John Stamos, Robin Mattson, Chris Robinson, and, of course, Anthony Geary and Genie Francis (Luke and Laura), whose steamy, but tumultuous, romance kept Xers chattering in the hallways at school and glued to their televisions five afternoons a week.

This early and frequent exposure to the consequences of relaxed programming standards has naturally affected the attitudes of this younger generation in regard to acceptable subject matter for television and other media. Television programmers today are frequently exhorted by broadcast reform groups to place a greater emphasis on "family values"—as if we finally realized what smut the little nippers have been watching all this time, and now that they are adults, we wonder whether we should be screening the programs they watch. For Generation X, that horse has already left the barn.

Stephen Boccho's 1994 series *NYPD Blue* elicited great concern from pressure groups like the American Family Association, who objected to the nudity, the graphic street language, and the violence. Yet, the program earned an impressive audience rating, despite threat of boycott and the reluctance of national advertisers to be identified with the controversial program.

Profanity, nudity, excessive violence, and graphic sexuality were rarities on television when Boomers were children. Today, all can be commonly found on both cable and network television. Made-for-television movies treat family violence, drug and alcohol addiction, rape, murder, incest, and worse. In one of the more interesting generational ironies, society's looser control over the content of the media and the greater emphasis on whatever "sells" can be traced historically to the more liberal politics of the Baby Boom and their strong emphasis on free expression and the freedom of the press/media. Now, many Boomers are deeply concerned over the effect on society (and children in particular) of such daily exposure to sex, violence, and profanity.

In a 1993 survey of public attitudes toward television, which was conducted by the Times-Mirror Center for People and the Press, adults under the age of thirty were significantly less likely to be offended by the depiction of sex and violence on television than were their elders.[4] (*Note*: People were scored according to how much violent entertainment they said they watched including fictional crime dramas, "real life" crime programs, and movies noted for their violence such as "Silence of the Lambs," "Blood Sport," etc. 45 percent of respondents fell within the "High" category for violence consumption, 35 percent in the "Average" category, and 20 percent in the "Low" category.)

Not only were younger adults less likely to believe that there is too much violence on television, but they also admit that they watch what violence is there. Asked to describe themselves as "heavy consumers" of violence, Generation X does so more frequently than either Boomers or older adults. (See Figure 6–3.)

As the real world for Xers becomes increasingly violent and frustrating, the Boomer public and Boomer advertisers try (vainly) to keep a lid on violence, sexual innuendo, and nudity in television. While Generation X is truly concerned about real-life violence, they are considerably more inured to violence in the media. (See Figure 6–4.)

Figure 6–3
Believe Entertainment TV
Is Too Violent

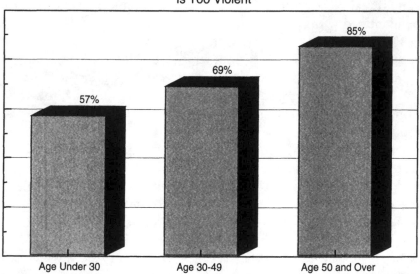

Source: Times Mirror Center for People and the Press, March 23, 1993

Figure 6–4
Heavy Consumers of
Violence on Television

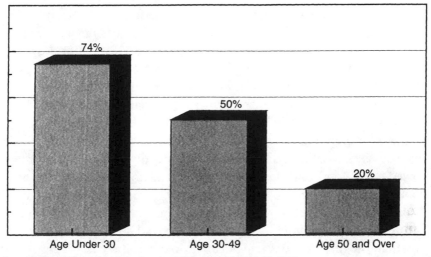

Source: Times Mirror Center for People and the Press, March 23, 1993

Boomers like to point out that Generation X often shares the same television programs, music, and entertainment that their parents enjoyed. "My kids still listen to the Grateful Dead," they say, as if this proves that we are all the same after all, and this so-called Generation Gap is just a figment of our collective imagination. "And all they watch on cable television are re-runs of the old network shows we used to see in the '70s."

But even when Xers share these interests with their parents, they probably see the shows we watched from a different point of view. Certainly, much of the "bite" is gone where the historical context is ancient history.

Sgt. Pepper's may once have been a lightning rod for the solidarity of a Western culture that was out to change the course of civilization, but for most young people today it's just one of many good, solid, classic-rock records. The music's onetime world-historical meanings have been stripped and replaced by fundamentally aesthetic ones.[5]

To Boomers, *All in the Family* demonstrated the triumph of the ideologically correct point of view, represented by Mike and Gloria, over the old-fashioned, bigoted, traditional views of Archie Bunker. Mike and Gloria had a modern marriage and a modern point of view about the role of women, child rearing, education, and politics. Boomers cheered when Mike and Gloria stood up for the new values. They identified with their lifestyle, their bell-bottoms, and their politics. Like many Boomer role models, Mike and Gloria were argumentative and confrontational. They disagreed on many issues, and eventually, they too separated and divorced.

But over the years, Archie Bunker and his ditsy, lovable wife Edith evolved as characters. Edith became wiser and stronger. Archie mellowed—still loud and stubborn, but soft-hearted, vulnerable, and sometimes not too old to learn a new trick. As Harry Castleman and Walter Podrazik point out, the Bunkers' marriage, with all its basic inequality and traditional role playing, proved stronger in the long run than the marriage of their Boomer offspring:

> Perhaps the most fascinating aspect of the series is watching it as a contrast in marriages between Archie and Edith's generation and Mike and Gloria's. This is something that can only be appreciated in reruns, because we can see the actions of the earlier episodes with the knowledge of how everything eventually does turn out. On that level, the older generation definitely "wins."[6]

As we have observed in earlier chapters, marriage and divorce are important themes to Generation X, while debates about civil rights and women's liberation are generally viewed as old news. Given the Bunker's ultimate faithfulness, and the Stivic's stubborn individuality, is it possible that Xers might fail to identify with Mike and Gloria and might secretly be rooting for Archie Bunker?

Then again, many Xers simply enjoy these nostalgic seventies sitcoms, the way a Boomer might enjoy a Laurel and Hardy movie. I once asked the son of an associate why he thought *The Brady Bunch* was so amusing. "Because," he answered, "they all had such incredibly bad perms!"

The late '70s and early '80s were the coming of age years, the teen years, for the earliest of Generation X. Although it happened to be a period of great international turmoil and domestic malaise, our Xers were understandably more concerned with dating, school, jobs, and college than they were with politics or economics.

> For us everything seemed normal. I remember wondering why people were surprised that prices were going up. I thought, that's what prices did. Some people were dismayed that America was losing the war in Vietnam, but to me it seemed like America had always been losing the war. Some people were scared that George Wallace was running for president, but he ran every time, didn't he?[7]

By 1981, the first Xers were twenty, but many were teenagers or younger and watching on their individual color television sets while Baby Boomers went crazy in the pursuit of cold cash. The 1980s, particularly as viewed through the media, had an alienating effect on Generation X and taught them much of what they think they know about Baby Boomers. Formerly idealistic and antiestablishment, Boomers had done an apparent about-face. As divorced mothers, hippy parents, or revered older siblings deserted Xer teens in droves to seek their fortune with big corporations or demanding entrepreneurial concerns, it represented to the younger generation another betrayal in a growing list. The media largely painted the decade of the 1980s as greedy, manipulative, and obsessed with money. To Xers, it also reeked with hypocrisy.

Perry Mason had become Arnie Becker, religious advice came from the Church Lady, and gentle, pot-smoking hippies were now the powerful drug lords of *Miami Vice*. Boomers were learning to play the game, and as was their wont, the game subsequently became everything. They engaged in the pursuit of the material with the same degree of excess that had characterized everything else they had attempted.

But Boomers and the media gave mixed messages, as greed was first exalted and then punished. Whether it was a fictional Gordon Gekko or a real-life Michael Millikin or Jim Bakker, in the end they suffered for their sins. As often as 1980s media was seduced by the glamour of the good life, the Baby Boomer's Judeo-Christian heritage would ultimately not allow really bad guys to finish first (at least not too often). So drug kingpins and gangsters had unhappy lives and were killed or jailed in the end. Ruthless and cruel CEOs lost their wives and their businesses, and bad girl executives were displaced by good, hard-working girls. The implications of these themes were not lost on Generation X.

In this context it is interesting to note the rise of Madonna during the 1980s. By proclaiming herself a "material girl," Madonna declared herself to Xers as both honest and naughty. In much the same way that James Dean's leather jacket spoke to previous generations, Madonna's straightforward materialism, and the success she enjoyed because of it, symbolized for Xers both a victory over the system and a parody of the values of their parents in the 1980s.

By consistently reinventing herself, often as a Boomer icon (Marilyn Monroe) or as a sex symbol, Madonna demonstrated that she could become whatever was necessary, and at the same time, she refused to be categorized. Madonna was successful in recognizing and reflecting Generation X's street-smart cynicism. If she seemed to be playing some game, it was a game that Generation X recognized: This is what it takes to be a superstar. Watch me do it. If Madonna's materialism seemed selfish to both generations, Xers also credited her for being strong, courageous, and honest about her selfishness. "It's like Madonna—she dresses like a whore, but she always knows what she wants."[8]

While superstars of other generations appeared artless—their screen persona often an extension of their real-life persona— Madonna reveled in contrivance and artificiality. She never hid the work she invested in her own success, but rather flaunted her myriad of disguises. Press releases revealed that she trained in the gym to enhance her figure, spent hours on makeup and wardrobe, and hired a personal trainer to prepare physically for the demands of a concert tour. She flaunted the dark roots of her bleached hair and wore her underwear on the outside. If you saw Madonna enjoying the fruits of her celebrity, you also saw her sweat to earn that celebrity, another demonstration whose implications were noted by Generation X.

By the end of the decade, the first of Generation X had finished their schooling and conceded that it would be necessary to work for a living and to play the game, as had every preceding Generation. But they had already rejected both the rabid idealism of the 1960s and the excessive materialism of the 1980s. Xers vowed they would not sell out their friends, families, or themselves in pursuit of a career, as Boomers had. Neither would they delude themselves that what they did for a living was more important than how they treated their neighbors or that the company they worked for deserved any special loyalty. Rather than seek meaning in their work, as Boomers did, Xers determined that work should not become more important than family or friends. They pragmatically sought the highest pay for the least-demanding occupations. They expected to be appreciated for their contributions, but they did not aspire to change the world. Rather, balance (regular hours, peer recognition, some time to themselves, and monetary compensation) became the key goal. Like Madonna, they would work, they would even work hard, but nobody would own them, and they would keep their souls.

The late 1980s also saw the introduction of the first of the so-called "tabloid television" shows, which quickly became the program wave of the early '90s. Local stations were looking to fill a void in their programming. Proliferating cable networks had started buying out whole studio inventories of movies. In doing so, they siphoned off a reliable source of cheap programming, leaving little for the local market. Many stations turned to cheap-to-produce, reality-based programming, like *Inside Edition* or *A Current Affair*.

The tabloid programs quickly developed a following among a variety of age groups, including Generation X. In fact, young adults watched these tabloid news shows as often as they watched the evening news and more often than they watched news in other dayparts. (See Figure 6–5.)

On the surface, these shows were modeled on newsmagazine formats, like *60 Minutes*, but the tabloids frequently relied on checkbook journalism, sensational reporting, reenactments of lurid crimes, and celebrity gossip to attract viewers and were immediately pounced upon by critics as pandering to our worst instincts. *A Current Affair* was the first. Hosted by Maurie Povich, *A Current Affair* was aired initially on New York station WNYW and later went to national distribution.

Perhaps the most infamous of their stories was aired during the course of the so-called "preppie murder" trial. A young New Yorker, Robert Chambers, was accused of murdering a young woman companion in Central Park, during an encounter involving "rough

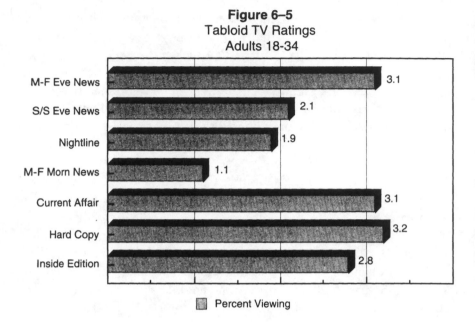

Figure 6–5
Tabloid TV Ratings
Adults 18-34

- M-F Eve News — 3.1
- S/S Eve News — 2.1
- Nightline — 1.9
- M-F Morn News — 1.1
- Current Affair — 3.1
- Hard Copy — 3.2
- Inside Edition — 2.8

Percent Viewing

Source: A.C. Nielsen: NTI Fourth Qtr 1991

sex." In an episode that became the prototype for tabloid reporting, *A Current Affair* obtained exclusive home video footage allegedly showing Chambers with a doll, apparently reenacting the crime, for the amusement of a group of young women at a party. He was subsequently convicted of the crime and sentenced to prison.

This formula was different in some important ways from the model for broadcast newsmagazines which prevailed during the '60s and '70s. First, the media were active participants in the stories they covered. Reporters on tabloid shows were encouraged to push the limits of investigative reporting and could be seen lying in ambush for alleged wrongdoers and grieving relatives alike. They arranged on-air confrontations between antagonistic parties or prepared elaborate sting operations to catch the perpetrators in the act of cheating, lying, or breaking the law. Far from the ideal of objective reporting, valued in the Boomer era, the tabloid newscaster would frequently involve himself and his program in such a way as to potentially alter the outcome of events as they were happening.

Tabloid programs also placed much more emphasis on interactivity with the viewing audience. They did phone polls, asking the public's opinion on the guilt or innocence of accused parties. They frequently solicited information from viewers, asking, "If you have any information about the events of this case, call our reporters. . . ." They frequently interviewed and speculated upon the testimony of peripheral characters like domestic workers, disgruntled employees, and neighbors. Often, these people had no information that would stand up to the rules of evidence, but they were presumed to contribute background information, which purported to help the public understand the true nature of the participants and the events that had ensued.

The viewers and the media were both participants in the tabloid story. Usually, they were partners, working together to bring out the truth. Sometimes, however, there was another whole element, in which the media themselves were revealed to have been duped or manipulated by one or more of the participants. Because the media were part of the story, and not just a venue through which the news was reported, they were themselves also fair game for the tabloid formula. Thus, the brawl between Geraldo Rivera and his talk-show panel of hate-mongering Skinheads became a bigger story than the Skinheads themselves. The widely reported sight of dashing, confrontational, investigative reporter Rivera with a huge bandage across his nose was eagerly seized by the mainstream news organizations and rehashed for weeks, in both print and electronic media.

This sort of incident appeals to the cynical nature of Generation X, who have recognized since their childhood the economic interests of the media and their close relationship to advertisers. To them, it's all about hype, anyway. Since they have never believed that the news is the objective truth, they also do not hold the news immune from the necessity to entertain.

As success spawned imitation, Tabloid Television mutated and prospered. Shows like *Unsolved Mysteries* and *Rescue 911* were not exactly news—and not exactly entertainment. Using celebrity hosts, like William Shatner and Robert Stack, they relied heavily on reenactments of events, often using the actual people involved in the incidents portrayed. But the important elements of sensational reporting, lurid crimes, innocents in danger, and ordinary people in heroic roles were carried over from the earlier tabloids.

It was a short step to news as pure entertainment. Made-for-television movies had always been a genre that drew inspiration from real-life events, but the race to translate major news stories to prime-time programming grew to a virtual feeding frenzy during the early 1990s. Perhaps the penultimate example of our appetite for the bizarre was the production in 1993 of, not one, but three made-for-network-television movies on the case of the so-called "Long Island Lollita," the Amy Fisher–Joey Buttafucco story, in which a teenaged Amy Fisher shot and wounded a Long Island housewife, Mary Jo Buttafucco, because of a sexual affair with her auto mechanic husband.

The story unfolded over many months with contradictory testimony, hidden videotapes and recordings, and ever more complicated twists of the plot. In the end, Amy was tried and convicted of attempted murder. Joey pled guilty to having sex with a minor and plea-bargained a short jail term. Mary Jo Buttafucco, after an initial wave of sympathy, was held up to public ridicule, and the tabloids did their best to force an estrangement from Joey, even arranging a televised session to confront Joey with his infidelity. In one rather noteworthy development, Geraldo Rivera held a "mock trial" of Joey Buttafucco, before any official charges had been brought against him. Ultimately Joey Buttafucco admitted the affair, which led to his subsequent imprisonment.

Finally, all three television networks announced plans to produce made-for-television versions of the story—two airing on the same night. All pretense to objectivity had been abandoned, and the ratings were very good.

ABC took another step into the brave new world of reality programming in mid-season 1990, building a half-hour prime-time show entirely around video taped by viewers: *America's Funniest Home Videos*. To the surprise of many Boomer advertisers, *Home Videos* became a smash hit in an otherwise unmemorable season.

And what could be tackier than home videos of unstaged amateurs slipping on banana peels, losing their pants, and being beat about the head by small children? The sequel: Home videos of *staged* events. People mugging for the camera, singing, telling jokes (badly), and dressing up in silly costumes. The predictable spin-off, *America's Funniest People*, was quickly launched, and the two programs were scheduled back to back for an uninterrupted hour of home movies on Sunday evening.

ABC's motivation was obvious: viewer video offered cheap programming in a time of escalating costs. And, Generation X liked these shows. *America's Funniest* consistently ranked among the top ten top-rated programs to adults 18–34. In fact, it ranked higher in this demographic than oft-cited Generation X programs like *Seinfeld* or *Northern Exposure*. (See Figure 6–6.)

As the young adults of Generation X increase in number, they begin to influence television ratings. And, as we all know, ratings determine programming. As Generation X increased their influence on the medium of television, the lines between news and entertainment became more and more blurred. Entertainment was about real-life events—silly ones, like we saw on "America's Funniest," or serious events, like those seen on the evening news.

Home video had also made its way into the evening news. Real-life dramas like the Rodney King beating or the riots in Los Angeles

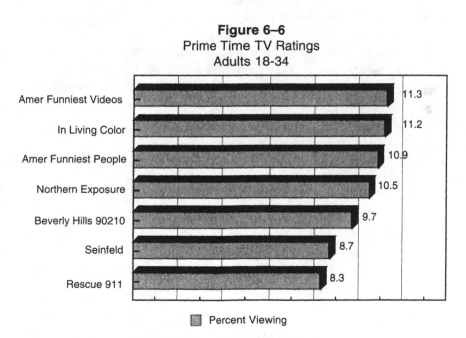

Figure 6–6
Prime Time TV Ratings
Adults 18-34

Source: A.C. Nielsen: NTI Fourth Quarter 1992

were reported by the common man. Any poor slob with a camera could bring the mighty down with videotaped evidence of misconduct. Any regular guy could witness a plane crash, a stirring rescue, or a violation of the building code and see his own "film at 11." Everyone was eligible for his own fifteen minutes of fame. All it took was access to a home video camera.

Video vigilantes sprung up in every community, as local stations offered cash for viewer video. It was a phenomenon that changed entirely the way news is reported in this country. In Boomer days, news media could be manipulated because there were a limited number of entities/channels through which news could be widely reported. This was particularly true in television, where the three networks dominated. But once the power to gather and frame the news was removed from the hands of a few, elite broadcasters, once it became anybody's job to see and report something interesting, it was no longer possible for the news to be controlled by any single interest group.

Generation X does not idealize, as Boomers do, the clear distinction between news and entertainment. They have observed since childhood the battle for ratings among local news broadcasters. They have seen the advertising campaigns. They have seen prime-time sit-coms interrupted for ten-second reports on real-life tragedies and recognized such bulletins as little more than commercials for the evening news. They have watched giggling reporters tell us that milk, or alcohol, or beef, or dieting, or anger is good for you—then bad for you—then not so bad after all.

Generation X has watched for years as Boomers have manipulated the media to reflect their point of view of the moment, even when it contradicts yesterday's point of view. News, to Generation X, is just more entertainment, except less trustworthy, because it purports to take itself seriously.

Tabloid programs, whether based on recent headlines, or pieced together from speculative historical accounts, or simply featuring videotape of real people falling over hoses and dancing with lampshades on their head, did not pretend to be "objective." They had a perspective and a point of view, and the perspective was that of *the audience*. In tabloid TV, viewers were allowed—no, encouraged—to participate. Viewers were also cameramen—who could show the world their own point of view—who could *be* part of the story.

Sure, tabloid shows were filled with hype and were less than well documented, but from an Xer point of view, all television was hype anyway. At least these shows were honest about it.

Generation X does not share the Baby Boom's idealism about the Fifth Estate. When it comes to journalism, they relish scandal and sensationalism. Tabloid reporting may not be as comforting, as reassuring as Peter Jennings, but it may ultimately prove to be more responsive to the needs of the people. News is entertainment. Entertainment is news.

7

Interactivity and
the New Media

Generation X is far more sophisticated about media than Boomers will ever be. This truth will be difficult for Boomer marketers to internalize, since Boomers have prided themselves since they were children on being "hip to media." Boomers learned early how to manage the network news and how to (sometimes) keep a show on the air, even though the networks wanted to cancel it. They know how to stage a press conference, how to ride the networks' coattails, and how to take advantage of audience segmentation to promote their products efficiently in the mass media.

But Boomer marketers have never had to deal with Generation X. Very little of what Boomers can do with media will have the desired effect on this audience:

> Exposed to consumerism and public relations strategies since we could open our eyes, we GenXers see through the clunky attempts to manipulate our opinions and assets, however shrinking. When we watch commercials, we ignore the product and instead deconstruct the marketing techniques. This is what we love about TV. We have learned that "content" means lies, and that in context lies brilliance.[1]

Xers know the salaries of the top NFL players, the demographic skew of their favorite sit-com, who owns the cable network, and how much money Pepsi fronted on the last Michael Jackson tour. They don't just admire a celebrity, they learn enough about him to debunk his claim to celebrity. Xers know the addresses of celebrity hairdressers and the phone numbers of their astrologers. In fact, the ocean of trivial information that is available about people like Madonna or Michael Jackson, for those who are interested enough to seek it out from tour films, documentaries, data bases, and fanzines, would send the average Boomer running for his fallout shelter.

How did Generation X get so smart about media? It started, of course, when they were children. We have already discussed the attraction of television for Generation X children, as well as their early disappointment with children's programming and commercialism. But television did not lose its fascination even though it was perceived as untrustworthy. Generation X learned to handle television like a team of lawyers handle a hostile witness—we did not raise a stupid generation here. The ground rules were established early: Generation X would take from the media what they needed and what they found entertaining, but they would never accept information from the media at face value. They would learn to be critical. They would learn to recognize hype, "weasel words," and exaggeration. And, like most good lawyers, they would always seek to control the communication.

Xers caught on quickly, partly because they spent a lot of time with electronic devices as children. Television was a compelling, sophisticated medium by the time the first Xers were born in 1961. Improved reception and quality of programming made it possible, if not desirable, to watch for twenty or more hours each day. Color television was the norm. By 1983, the number of channels received by the average household was ten or eleven. Two years later, that number had doubled. Today the average household can receive over thirty-five channels, and the number is still growing. (See Figure 7–1.)

Personal computers were encountered in school, and in affluent circles they were being promoted as the latest household appliance, although they were still unwieldy gadgets with limited usefulness. Primitive electronic games, some of which could be displayed on the television screen or computer monitor, were available before the first Xers were out of grade school.

Generation X, approaching the new electronic gadgets without any preconceived ideas about what television or video games were supposed to do and without much regard for how expensive the

Figure 7–1
Number of Channels Received
By Average U.S. Household

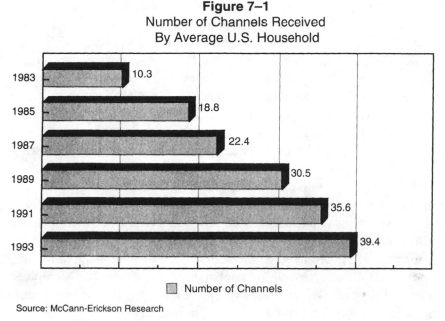

Source: McCann-Erickson Research

A.C. Nielsen

equipment was, often proved more adept than their parents who were more hesitant and more tentative. Does there exist in America today a self-respecting eight-year-old who cannot slam-dunk both his parents at a game of *Mario Bros?* Of course not.

The media are a source of many kinds of information and education. Xers learned to read with Big Bird, learned to Moonwalk with Michael, and learned about sex from Luke and Laura. Marketing and public relations were not difficult either. Hours of commercial television time are made available every week for documentary treatments of people, famous or not so famous, doing whatever it is they do. One can see Michael Jackson making videos or watch Paul McCartney taping a concert with behind-the-scenes vignettes. If you are interested, you can watch professional models doing a photo layout for *Sports Illustrated's* Swimsuit Issue or learn what goes into a successful commercial. At best, such documentaries are trivia background for hard-core fans; at worst they are blatantly designed to add hype to a commercial venture. But Generation X watches them and learns.

Then there are the consumer guides to media: *E!*, MTV, *Entertainment Tonight* and magazines like *Premiere, Billboard, Entertainment Weekly, Rolling Stone, Interview, People, Us,* and *TV Guide,* which devote much of their content to the business basis and marketing strategies of books, music, movies, and broadcasting. Most of these vehicles skew to younger audiences because Xers are disproportionately interested in how the media works. Just as earlier generations took cars and trucks apart to dissect their engines and learn their secrets, Generation X examines commercials, cartoons, and prime-time movies. If school was boring, television seldom was.

Now, with the help of constantly improving technology, Xers are media connoisseurs, who can and do browse the electronic landscape, selecting what interests them most. When there were only three or four channels, television had no time available for obscure programs not guaranteed to attract large audiences. The least common denominator determined what one could watch. Documentaries of people taking pictures of movie stars was one of many subjects television abdicated to the fan magazines. In today's multichannel environment, however, the challenge is more likely to be where to get enough programming to fill up all those hours of potential viewing. The solution for the networks is often to air inexpensive or free programming, produced by someone with a commercial purpose in mind. Today, when anyone makes a movie, somebody makes a movie about making the movie. When an advertiser shoots a new commercial campaign, someone is likely to make a documentary about the process. And when a superstar goes on tour . . . well, you get the idea.

But there is something in the psyche of Generation X that is comfortable being once or twice removed from reality. The process becomes the product as one watches a movie on television about making a video. The video is itself, a commercial for a compact disc, which is a recording of a live performance. MTV specializes in just this sort of thing, and the fondness of Generation X for MTV is legendary.

It also helps explain how they find this stuff. For most self-respecting Xers, MTV is where you go when the commercials come on. Contrary to popular opinion, MTV's quick-cut, fast-fade format is attractive to Xers not because they have short attention spans but because one can see a whole segment within the confines of a network or cable commercial break. Xers were among the first to realize the true value of the remote control.

"Control" is the key word. Far from being passive viewers of television, Xers are active channel surfers, who view with remote control in hand, searching among hundreds of options for whatever suits the impulse of the moment. They select among broadcast programs, cable, prerecorded videos rented from the store, shows they taped earlier in the week, and video games, without discriminating by source. They could care less whether Fox is a "real" network or whether the program was taped by them or by the video distributor. If they like the content of the show, they will watch. They have no loyalty to networks, either cable or broadcast, since networks mean nothing to the consumer. Programming dictates selection.

The remote control explains how obscure little programs, like *Ren and Stimpy* or *Beavis and Butthead*, can become major X fads, while remaining relatively unknown among Boomers and others.

Ren and Stimpy were a favorite of Generation X, at least until they were "discovered."

While Boomers were the driving force behind the growth of color and multiple sets, Xers were the impetus for multiple channels, cable, and VCRs. Not content to choose between Monday Night Football and sit-coms about aging single mothers, Xers also wanted their MTV, their Luke and Laura, their *Nick at Night*, their *Wayne's World*, their *Mario Bros.* Overworked parents indulged them as often as possible, even in less affluent families, since video games, cable, and Blockbuster Video were cost-effective (and safer) alternatives to more expensive entertainment.

Improvements in color broadcasting and multiset households grew dramatically during the 1970s, when Xers were still young children, and we have described the events that set the stage for this burst in technology. But Boomers did not carry the technology to the limit of its capability. They did not proceed to demand multiple-channel access, and they did not create a strong market for VCRs until Generation X began to insist on them—right about the time the first Xers moved off to college.

I remember vividly the day my Generation X niece, Sandy, came for a late-summer visit before starting her freshman term at a Southern university. Knowing full well how college expenses can stress the family budget, I asked her whether there was still something she needed for her dorm room that I could supply as a gift. I expected to hear that she wanted a certain textbook or perhaps a special desk chair. She said what she really needed was a VCR, since she hated to miss her soap operas while she was in class. "I have a television," she said, "but Mom won't let me take the VCR up to school." Like many Boomers, I had recently bought my first VCR and was still luxuriating in my newfound status among the electronic avant-garde. To Sandy, the VCR was already a necessity.

It was not that the technology was unavailable to Boomers. In some cases the technology had existed for decades, but it was not in common use because the average viewer was unable and/or unwilling to pay for it. Boomers, as a group, turned their noses up at VCRs and multiple channels. Even today, when cable television and VCRs are commonly found in Boomer households, the average thirty-five to fifty-year-old barely taps their potential. I know many intelligent adults who freely admit they cannot set the clock on their video system.

In the 1980s, Boomers were still content to passively view whatever the networks offered. It is often said, in this decade of the "information highway" and 500-channel capacity, that technology will change our lives. While I do not dispute that technology changes our lives, I do think that sometimes we get it backwards. The development of technology does not change the way people think and act, unless people want it to. Rather, *people inspire the creation of technological development by providing a market for it.* The VCR is a good example. The technology was there, but early VCRs sat on the shelf until Generation X saw a need for them. Once VCR technology had been adopted by Xers, once the market was created, VCR technology responded with improved product to supply that market.

It wasn't until the 1980s that VCRs and cable television really took off, fueled by Generation X's desire to control their media environment. When college and jobs began to interfere with viewing their favorite soaps, many Xers looked for logical alternatives to the networks' traditional scheduling patterns. They discovered time shifting through VCRs, that is, taping a show to view later. Leading-edge Xers were entering their twenties, and many took VCRs off to college with them or installed them (along with cable and other enhancements) in their parents' households. Affluent Boomers were willing to spend, especially for their children, and as the market grew, the technology quickly improved. The price of VCRs came tumbling down, and that spurred expansion into less affluent markets. Just as in the '60s one could often see a television antenna jutting from the rooftop of the poorest cabin in Appalachia, in the early '90s one could find a video cassette player in eight out of ten American households.

As middle-aged Boomers opened up their collective checkbook, Xers acted as electronic consultants, and electronic technology blossomed. Home came VCRs, satellite dishes, cable television, and multichannel capabilities. In the affluent household, the "living room" was replaced by the "video center." Even in poorer neighborhoods, many bedrooms had their own collection of new electronic equipment.

The number of households with VCRs grew from less than 6 percent in the early '80s to almost 80 percent today. Xers saw the potential of the new electronic media long before Boomers did. (See Figure 7–2.)

Once VCRs became common, the evolution of video stores like Blockbuster Video was not far behind. Video rentals changed the

Figure 7–2
VCR Growth
Percent Households

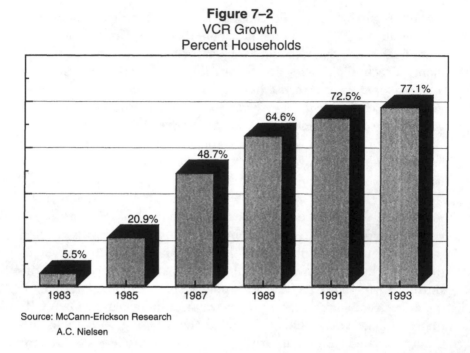

Source: McCann-Erickson Research
A.C. Nielsen

nature of the film distribution industry by offering an alternative revenue stream (the rental market) to producers. This gives each film a longer life span and a greater potential to generate revenue. Because the filmmaker has a broader window of opportunity to recoup his costs and generate a profit, it becomes more economically feasible to produce films with relatively smaller audience potential.

Access to feature films at home created additional competition for television and helped to spur the growth of cable. The new market and the clear demand for feature films, pay-per-view events, and specials attracted investors and operators who began negotiating in virtually every municipality to "lay the wire" and to provide cable access to every household. As cable movies competed with feature films, many rental movie distributors diversified their product line to include video games, which stimulated additional growth in that industry. Remote-control devices were improved to handle multiple media. The new entertainment options spurred the public to upgrade their television and other electronic equipment, and so on.

Generation X just wanted to view what they wished, when they wished. They were willing and able to invest the time to learn how to accomplish this and, in the process, provided a market, which stimulated research, which resulted in new and better product. Thus, as soon as Generation X learned to operate "Pong" from a remote-control joystick, the scene was set for the next technological leap in media.

As for Boomers, it is not uncommon, as people get older, to reach a technology "saturation point." After all, how many channels does one television viewer need anyway? How often can one replace his/her personal computer, stereo, television, telephone, and so on, just because there is a new and better model for sale? Boomers were perfectly happy to add cable to their existing sets, and maybe even a VCR—but only if the kids would use it. Personal computers were another matter entirely. Most Boomers were uneasy about computers, although many were required to learn computer basics at work. Left alone, many Boomers had reached the technology saturation point by the mid-1980s. At that point, Boomers were no longer seeking new technology, although many continued to adopt it as it became available.

Generation X first encountered computers in grade school, and many Xers were on-line before their parents had even heard of computer networks. Xers became conversant with computer technology at school and practiced their skills in video arcades, with "Atari" and "Nintendo" and with the earliest Apple home computers. For these kids, programming the VCR was a snap. And far from being enchanted under the Orwellian spell of the mass media, Xers quickly discovered that television was one of the few things in their lives that they could *control*.

My young nephew Andy, aged eleven, after seeing that cinematic classic *Beetlejuice* was walking around the house humming "Day-O," the old Harry Belafonte song. My sister thought to impress him by digging out the old record and playing it for him. Andy was impressed; in fact, he was thrilled and wanted to hear the song played over and over again. After the first few replays, Maggie left him alone with his newly discovered music, only to be called back into the room each time the song ended. Finally Andy sensed her patience was wearing thin and offered, "Mom, if you would just show me where the rewind button is, you wouldn't have to keep coming in here." The boy had never seen a record played. He wasn't deprived or slow. He was just used to playing his own music on his own Walkman or listening to Compact Discs, and he didn't know that records don't rewind.

This "rewind phenomenon" is in fact a common behavior in '90s children. My own children and grandchildren play and replay favorite parts of favorite movies until their parents run screaming from the room. My son, Wayne, at age four or five was particularly fond of replaying scenes from movies that frightened him until he was not frightened any more.

If Boomers view television from a passive state of mind, Xers have a more *organic* relationship with the media. Far from the short attention span they have been labeled with, Xers can turn a two-hour movie into a five-hour immersion in film, by rewinding, re-viewing, and stopping for snack breaks. They are also capable of processing information from multiple channels simultaneously. Yes, they *can* watch television, talk on the telephone, and do their homework all at the same time. Channel surfing with a remote control is not unlike skimming a book—or like skimming fifty books at once. One's attention is focused on the medium, but with an ulterior purpose, and if the medium does not respond with entertainment or involving information, it is quickly discarded in favor of more fruitful pastures. But in the process, the surfer absorbs some information from each screen. The sum total may give an entirely different perspective than any individual program, but information is gleaned nonetheless.

In every media variety, Xers have been pushing the envelope toward interactivity and away from mass communication since they first discovered how to turn on the television set. While Boomers and older generations often perceive technology as dehumanizing, too big, and too mechanized to deal with, Generation X has been quietly finding ways to personalize technology as it develops.

Xers provided an audience for tabloid TV and reality-based television movies and are helping to move information of all kinds from the domain of the elite to the province of the people. They are responsible for the growth in popularity of small metropolitan newspapers, which build their reader base on entertainment listings, movie reviews, and personal ads.

As we have seen, they stimulated the growth of multiple channels in television. They caused the boom in VCRs. They are the force behind Blockbuster Video. They are the voice of the Internet and America On-Line and hundreds of chat lines, Local Area Networks (LANs), Wide Area Networks (WANs), and Multi User Domains (MUDs).

"I am on the cusp of Generation X," admits Tim Disney, thirty-four-year-old virtual reality pioneer and grandson of Walt. "Mine was the last college class for which computers were not a degree *requirement*."

After college, as private enterprise began to adopt computer technology in the workplace, Generation X had even better access to new electronic equipment as well as advanced training in software and programming. Boomer managers tended to view computers as word processors or glorified typewriters. As such, they assigned the new computer to the lowest ranking, and youngest, of the staff—often the clerk, trainee, or secretary. This is remarkable when you consider that more familiar technology, like a compact refrigerator or a portable telephone, would invariably be coopted first by officers of the company. But computers went to the rank and file. Because Boomers largely failed to perceive the true nature and potential of computers, they literally pushed the technology off on the next generation and, in doing so, sometimes sowed the seeds of their own obsolescence.

If your office, like mine, has voicemail or E-mail or both, it may surprise you to learn that people under age thirty-five use these communications options in a very different way than people over thirty-five. To most Boomers, voicemail is the devil's own invention. When a Boomer dials your number she hopes to hear your actual human voice answer the telephone. When she hears instead a recorded message, she may hang up or leave a number to call, but either way, she will be frustrated at having missed the personal connection.

A Boomer deals with her own voicemail or answering machine by basically ignoring it. Virtually every Boomer I know uses the same message on his/her own home or office answering machine. This message was probably recorded the day the machine was installed and has never been altered, even a little:

This is 555–2222. I'm sorry that I'm not available to take your call right now, but if you leave your name and number I'll call you back as soon as possible.

Generation X thinks Boomers are totally clueless about voicemail. First of all, if you program your machine to reveal absolutely nothing about your personal identity, whereabouts, schedule, or state of mind, how does the caller begin to guess how to phrase a message for you? Recognizing security concerns, it is often still possible to let your callers know that you are on vacation and not in the office, or that you will be checking messages after 3:00 P.M. Many Xers put a lot of time and thought into keeping their voicemail greeting fresh and relevant, and this requires ongoing attention to what comes in and what goes out, and how the message device works.

When you leave a message on an answering machine, Xers will tell you it is not helpful to say, "Please call me at 555–2222." The idea, instead, is to communicate what you called about, like "Are you free for lunch on the 27th?" In this way, they point out, when your associate returns the call and gets your machine, he can say, "The 27th looks good. Meet you at the usual place, 12 sharp."

This is called communication. Generation X does it well; Boomers are hopeless and are therefore much more likely to get caught in endless rounds of "phone tag," which contribute nothing to their understanding and confirm their already negative opinions of voicemail.

Most Boomers, including me, view voicemail with suspicion and hostility, and we cannot therefore conceive its use as a flexible communications tool. And while we fight the technological shift and complain bitterly about its limitations, our Xer neighbors are busily using it to communicate in all sorts of innovative ways.

I, myself, am hopeless. I employ a live, human assistant who answers my telephone, fields routine requests, and writes down messages on little slips of paper. This makes me and my Boomer clients feel better. However, when my Xer daughter calls, she will often ask my live assistant to transfer her to my voicemail so that I can hear her message in a more personal way in her own voice. In one office I visit, the younger workers sometimes record the latest hit song on voicemail and send it around to one another to lighten the day. A young agency associate, who had recently been promoted, dealt with the onslaught of congratulatory phone calls by programming his phone to say:

Now that I'm a Veep, leave a message at the beep.

The same associate wrote an enlightening article about the use of voicemail for the Detroit media sales community, which was published in the Magazine Representatives' monthly newsletter. I would have thought it impossible to find enough to say on the subject to make an article, but I was both interested and enlightened to read his perspective on the subject.

By contrast, I once arrived home at about midnight to find a message from my Boomer sister which said:

This is your sister. C'mon Karen, I know you're there. Just pick up the damn phone for a minute, because I want to tell you something. [Pause] Ok, then, Goodbye.

E-mail is another medium Xers understand. From joke-of-the-day clubs to the distribution of underground music on the Internet, Generation X will explore the limits of the system and push it to do more. In most large companies with E-mail, special user lists, created by and for the younger staff, provide a method for Xers to wisecrack on the topic of the day, safe from the eyes of management. Office gossip and rumors spread with a rapidity that managers find startling, because they are instantaneously transmitted to multiple parties over the E-mail network. The water cooler has been replaced by the much more efficient computer screen, and most Boomers haven't even noticed.

Xers use technology to personalize and humanize everything they touch, demanding only that hype and commercialism be kept in check. They will be the first generation to realize the potential marriage between television and the computer. They are already heavily immersed in communication through computer networks, they understand being "wired," and because of Xers, interactive television is just around the corner.

Interactive television is actually a misnomer, since interactivity will ultimately require the combined resources of three streams of present-day technology: television, telephone, and the personal computer. The essential technology that has made the next generation of electronic communications possible is digitalization. At its most basic, digitalization is the reduction of data to a series of digits (ones and zeros) which can be "read" by a computer. Because these digits can be compressed quite efficiently, we can now read and store vast amounts of data on relatively small (compact) media discs. This makes it possible to read and to store color graphics, including moving pictures, voices, and other images, which, in the past, would have required huge and unwieldy banks of information. In the past, it was impractical for home or office computers and totally out of reach for everyday appliances like telephones or televisions to store or to transmit such huge masses of data.

The next breakthrough was fiberoptic cable, which can be used to transmit digitalized information in virtually unlimited quantity. Together, these technologies have the potential to completely change the face of communications in America and around the world.

Where Boomers cannot conceive the potential of interactive television, Xers have been waiting for the technology to accomplish what they have already conceived. Interactivity will put control into the hands of the consumer to a greater degree than ever possible in pure broadcast television. For example, since huge data bases can be stored, it will be possible to digitalize full-length motion pictures and make them available to the consumer on demand. No longer will the viewer need to make an appointment to see a movie on television. He can cue it up at his leisure without going to the video store.

The same may be true, eventually, for episodes of the leading prime-time programs. Today, if the viewer misses *Roseanne* on Tuesday night, he or she is just plain out of luck for that episode, until the network schedules a rerun. With interactive television, it is theoretically possible that the viewer could watch his/her favorite show on any night of the week, or any day for that matter. If an episode were missed or if you just wanted to see it again, you could call it up out of the archives and watch it as often as you liked.

For advertisers, it is the two-way communication potential of interactive television that is most intriguing. Because digitalized data travels by "wire" (by fiberoptic cable in most cases), it is as easy to send a message back as it is to send a message out. Thus, if the viewer desires more information about a product seen on television, he or she has the means to request more information, to ask for a coupon, or, in some cases, to order the product directly from the manufacturer.

The same principle will allow personal communication between households with interactive sets. As part of an interactive television hookup, each subscriber may be given a cellular telephone. That telephone will work through the same fiberoptic cable links employed by the television system to reach any other telephone in the market. That makes it possible to carry the phone (and the phone number) with you as you go about your business anywhere in the market. Whether you are at work, at home, in your car, or shopping at the mall, it will be possible to reach you by telephone at the same number.

It is not unlikely that, in the near future, the average household will have a central communications center that incorporates what is now the television set with the personal home computer and the telephone, which will have video as well as audio communication capacity. Each individual might have his own telephone number, which is issued like a social security number and stays with him throughout his life span.

Since an interactive television will require a computer to read data and a keyboard, mouse, or other input device for the viewer to communicate with the system, it will be a short step to the incorporation of all those programs now housed in the personal computer. Banking, shopping, budget programs, educational software, video games, and the like will eventually reside in a single communications device. If this sounds like science fiction, it is not. The technology is available today.

It will naturally take a few years to rewire the country with fiberoptics, but that has begun. It will take time to refine the technology and to develop the software. But interactive will be established in some U.S. markets in less than two years.

And interactive will be disproportionately adopted by Generation X. Xers, not Boomers, will be furnishing newly formed households. They will be the primary purchasers of new electronic systems from the mid-1990s until 2010. And that may be very bad news for traditional marketers.

The more that control rests in the hands of the consumer, the more difficult it will be to expose that consumer to a traditional advertising message. Remote controls and channel surfing interrupt commercial viewing. Pay-per-view, premium cable networks, and most home video already allow the viewer to completely bypass commercial interruptions. Whenever the least hint of commercialism has intruded upon the Internet, the reaction has been extremely negative. Our challenge as marketers in the years 1995 and beyond will be to find ways to communicate useful and meaningful information about products and services, without assuming that we can *intrude* those messages upon a passive audience. Instead, we must be *invited* by a knowledgeable consumer to impart the information he seeks, at the moment he is willing to listen. This is a very different proposition than the discipline of advertising as it exists today.

As control shifts away from the media and into the hands of the consumer, a new generation awaits the advertising message, with remote control in hand and cynicism in his heart.

8

Consumer Behavior

Choosing Brand X

G eneration X reports itself to be less loyal to brands than Baby Boomers. When Simmons asked in its 1993 survey, young adults reported that they were less likely to look for brand names when shopping. They were also more open to experimenting with new brands. In general, brand loyalty tended to increase with education. In both generations, the most brand-loyal were people with college degrees; the least brand-loyal were those with high school diplomas or less. (See Figure 8–1.)

Among college-graduate Boomers and Xers, reported brand loyalty was virtually identical. However, there was a significant difference in the attitudes of Boomers and Generation X in the middle educational ranges, and Xers who did not graduate high school showed markedly lower brand loyalty. Brand switching was also more frequently reported by Xers in all segments except those with college degrees. (See Figure 8–2.)

A number of factors might have contributed to this. First of all, Generation X has always had the opportunity to choose from a wider variety of brands. The supermarket shelves carry a much wider variety of product today, thanks to the continued growth of cheap and efficient transportation. Even in remote or less affluent areas, the number of brand choices has increased significantly since the '60s and '70s.

And, as we have seen, most advertisers have not targeted Generation X adults in their marketing efforts. As children, they saw

Figure 8–1
I Always Look for the Brand Name on the Package
(Agree A Lot)

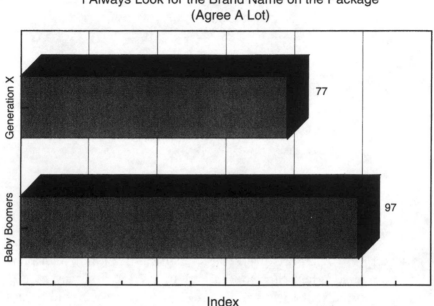

Index

Source: Simmons Market Research Bureau:
1993 Study of Media and Markets

more commercials than did other generations, primarily for toys, cereals, and vitamins. But over the past decade, many major advertisers have shifted away from brand advertising (which encourages brand loyalty) toward price promotion (which encourages brand switching). The smaller portion of advertising dollars dedicated to brand advertising has primarily been targeted toward the ever-popular Baby Boomer. Although many Xers have been shoppers since they were children, very little effort has been made to cultivate them as brand-loyal consumers, and therefore, we should not be surprised to learn that they now feel less loyalty to major brands.

Generation X may also simply be exhibiting the independence of the young. As less experienced consumers, they can be expected to experiment more. In the natural process of learning, young adults try out alternatives, test new brands, and discard others. Later, they may learn that certain brands are reliable choices and settle into a more predictable shopping pattern. The fact that college-educated

Figure 8–2
I Like to Change Brands Often for the Sake of
(Agree A Lot)

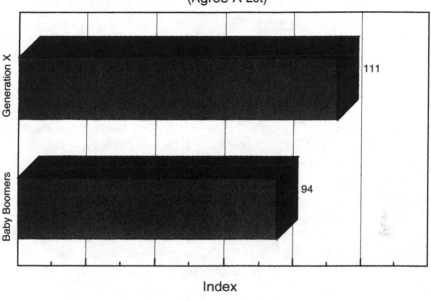

Index

Source: Simmons Market Research Bureau:
1993 Study of Media and Markets

Xers admit a more brand-loyal pattern would tend to bear this out. Those with college degrees are older than those with high school or some college (in this age group, they may not have finished their education yet). Younger Xers may be still experimenting, while older Xers, having learned from their experience, are settled into a more brand-loyal pattern.

To help us understand the responses of these younger Xers, it may be useful to take a look at research conducted in 1993 by DYG, Inc for *Men's Health* magazine. Comparing groups of men by age, *Men's Health* compared men over age 46 to men aged 30–45 and to men 18–29. Adhering to the more traditional definition of Baby Boomers, these age groupings/labels are different from those used throughout this book, but the trends are directional.

This research found a natural progression of values with evolutionary movement from one generation to the next. But the researchers were surprised at how often a different pattern emerged.

Often, the 30–45-year-old group exhibited an aberrant trend, while young Xers (18–29) more closely resembled older men (46+). Boomers, as we have seen already, are more comfortable with their own personal definition of success and more likely to be risk takers than either of the two other groups.

Often, Xers showed a more conservative, conforming pattern than did Boomers. While Boomers have long prided themselves on their nonconformity and independent thinking, Generation X admits that they care what other people think. (See Figure 8–3.)

Conformity, especially to the strivers among Generation X, does not represent blind adherence to the standards of a huge, homogeneous mass. It is less the style of *The Man in the Grey Flannel Suit* and more the style of Tom Cruise in the movie *The Firm.* Generation X is street-smart and hungry and making an effort to fit the norm for a specific, selected group, in order to achieve the goal of comfort or wealth or influence. They believe it is necessary to adopt appropriate behaviors if one wants to get ahead. But they do not believe it necessary to internalize the behaviors they may

Figure 8–3
My Sense of Success Comes from the Way I Feel
About Myself, Not What Others Think

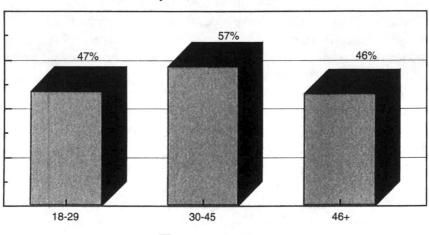

Source: Manscan: Three Generations of Men, a proprietary research study
sponsored by Men's Health Magazine and conducted by DYG, Inc.

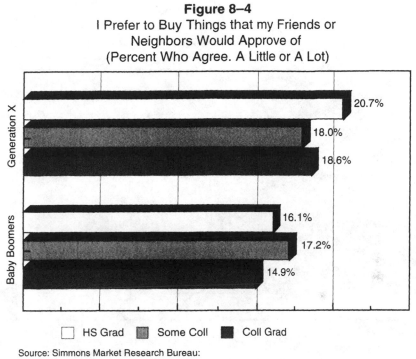

Figure 8–4
I Prefer to Buy Things that my Friends or
Neighbors Would Approve of
(Percent Who Agree. A Little or A Lot)

Source: Simmons Market Research Bureau:
1993 Study of Media and Markets

adopt—like Tom Cruise, they can break from the pack at any time, whenever it is in their self-interest to do so.

In this generation of greater social and ethnic diversity, it is also appropriate to ask, "Conformity to what?" For some Xers, conformity may involve issues of loyalty to family or ethnic heritage. For others, it may be the observance of social customs evolved among their peer group. One may signal his allegiance to the group by wearing baggy jeans, a baseball cap, and high-top sneakers. Another may express the same desire to fit in with Spandex shorts and roller blades. (See Figure 8–4.)

There is more than a little irony here. For Generation X, diversity values conformity. Despite differing social, economic, and cultural backgrounds, Xers recognize the common needs of their peers to be successful, to value their heritage, to be a part of their chosen group. Boomers at the same age raised angry fists in defense of nonconformity, all the while dressed in the identical, obligatory bell-bottoms, flowered shirts, and long hair.

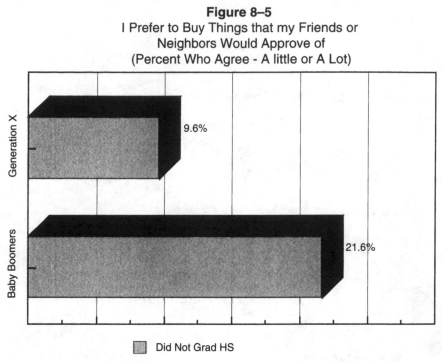

Figure 8–5
I Prefer to Buy Things that my Friends or
Neighbors Would Approve of
(Percent Who Agree - A little or A Lot)

Did Not Grad HS

Source: Simmons Market Research Bureau:
1993 Study of Media and Markets

There is at least one important exception to this trend. The youngest and least-educated segment of Generation X (those who have not graduated high school) actively rejects status through material possessions. Unlike their older brothers and sisters, they do not seek approval through the purchase of branded products. Given the fact that this segment includes those who are least able to afford to purchase what they see advertised, this may reflect a greater alienation of the least affluent segment of the generation and the increasing gap, in attitudes as well as affluence, between the privileged and the poor. (See Figure 8–5.)

Meanwhile, the best-educated and most affluent of Generation X chooses to fit in, to play it safe in order to achieve what they want and need out of life. They may view it as a fundamental issue of survival. (See Figure 8–6.)

Even though Generation X perceives itself to be unaffected by brands, even disdainful of them, the data indicate that some seg-

Figure 8–6
These Days, in Order to Get What You Want Out of
Life, You've Got to Play it Safe

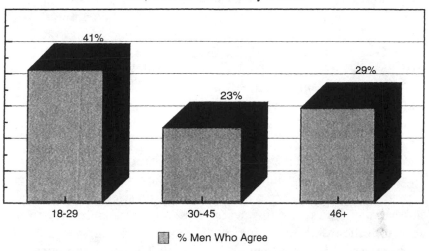

☐ % Men Who Agree

Source: Manscan: "Three Generations of Men" a proprietary research study
sponsored by Men's Health Magazine and conducted by DYG, Inc.

ments of the generation are indeed loyal, at least sometimes. And the experience of certain marketers bears this out. The success of brands like Nike, Doc Martin, The Gap, Saturn, and others should not be overlooked. We know that some Xers can be fiercely attached to brands that have earned their interest and attention. Furthermore, once they have made a commitment to a brand decision, it may be very difficult to get their attention on behalf of any other product. The Generation X dislike of advertising and hype can make it difficult to convince them to consider an alternative.

A question commonly asked by Boomer marketers about Generation X is this: Are they really that different? Recognizing all that has been said about demographic trends, the history of the media, attitudes, and lifestyles . . . so what? If they come to the department store or to the showroom floor with a different set of life experiences, does it really change what they purchase or how they arrive at their purchase decision? When all is said and done, does Generation X really behave differently in the aisle of the supermarket?

There is no easy answer to that question. Generation X, like every large body of consumers, is a study in contradictions. Sometimes, they go their own way. Sometimes, they act just like every-body else. But whatever they do, in the supermarket, on the street, or at home, they do for reasons shaped by their generation's experience with the media, with its peers, and with its community. And this is the key to understanding their marketplace behavior. Even when Generation X acts just like the Baby Boomers, the motivation may be very different. And, just when you think you've got them all figured out, they will do something that surprises you.

If there are any rules for marketing to Generation X, this is rule number one: *Never assume they are the same as Boomers—even when they look the same.*

Environmentalism is a good example. It has been widely reported that Generation X is concerned about the environment and that environmental concerns often guide them in the selection of products and services. Intuitively, this makes sense. It seems logical that Xers, to whom the task of cleaning up the planet will largely fall, would be even more dedicated about preserving resources and even less tolerant of pollution than older generations. Marketers like Fort Howard Corporation, The Body Shop, Benetton, and many others actively promote the "environmentally friendly" aspects of their products or services on the assumption that their target audiences care enough about these issues to change their buying behavior or, in some cases, to pay more for the product that does not pollute.

In fact, research suggests that environmentalism is more important to Baby Boomers than to Generation X—at least, as a factor in purchase decisions. Bearing in mind that *nobody* is in favor of destroying the atmosphere, polluting the water supply, or living in a solid waste dump, Boomers are more likely to demonstrate concern by purchasing products marketed as "environmentally friendly."

In general, Generation X reports that they prefer products that are recycled or that use recycled packaging. But they are no more likely to report this behavior than is the average U.S. adult and are less likely than Baby Boomers to use recycled products. In part, this is a reflection of their lower income and more cautious shopping habits. But the small difference in price for recycled paper products does not entirely account for their reluctance. Remember, this is a consumer group that regularly pays a premium price for branded sneakers and blue jeans. (See Figure 8–7.)

It's not that Generation X doesn't care about the environment,

Figure 8–7
I Buy Products that Use Recycled Paper in Their
Packaging (% College Grads who agree)

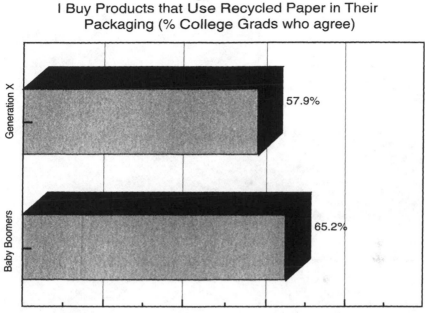

Source: Simmons Market Research Bureau:
1993 Study of Media and Markets

either. Often, their assessment of the state of the planet is bleaker and more pessimistic than that of older adults. But, many Xers think of environmental problems as too large, too complex for one individual to deal with. In focus groups, they are likely to shrug their shoulders, sigh, and admit that they do not feel empowered to make an impact. The feeling that "you can't do anything about it anyway" may contribute to a sense of fatalism, a sense that any action would ultimately be futile.

Then there is that famous Generation X skepticism. Who do you believe? How do you know that an advertiser who claims his products are safer is not concealing something or ignorant of an element that will ultimately turn out to be worse than what we have now. Or perhaps the manufacturer is simply lying. Xers are not usually inclined to accept advertising claims alone as proof of real environmental safety.

Xers seem to be willing to recycle, because that is something tangible that an individual can do. But they clearly differentiate be-

Figure 8–8
I Buy Products (Napkins, Towels, Toilet Paper, etc.)
that are Recycled (percent who agree)

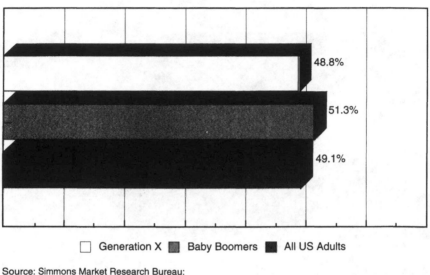

☐ Generation X ▨ Baby Boomers ■ All US Adults

Source: Simmons Market Research Bureau:
1993 Study of Media and Markets

tween the act of recycling and the purchase of "recycled" products. They are slightly more cautious than Boomers about investing their personal money in products or product packaging that claims to have been recycled. (See Figure 8–8.)

As to the fundamental issues, Xers are a lot less likely than Baby Boomers to believe in an easy solution to the problem. Remember, Boomers are idealists; Generation X is much more pragmatic. Simmons Market Research Bureau asked adults of all ages whether they agreed with the statement "All products that pollute the environment should be banned." Baby Boomers were more likely to agree. (See Figure 8–9.)

When we isolate college graduates in each generation, the difference is even more striking. While more than half of Boomer graduates agreed (a lot or a little) with the statement "All products that pollute the environment should be banned," only one-third of Generation X graduates agreed. This is important, because just as college graduates ultimately comprise the most affluent market segments, they will also be our most important and influential

Figure 8–9
All Products that Pollute the Environment
Should be Banned (percent who agree)

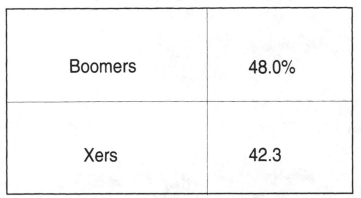

| Boomers | 48.0% |
| Xers | 42.3 |

Source: Simmons Marker Research Bureau:
1993 Study of Media and Markets

resources as we confront the issues of environmental preservation in the future. (See Figure 8–10.)

Yankelovich Partners found a similar pattern of responses on issues of environmental protection in the 1992 Monitor.

Boomers are confident of their ability to judge and are inured to slogans as a rallying point—even on complex issues. But Generation X is less sure they know the answer. In fact, the more educated they are, the less likely they are to accept the easy, obvious solution as the correct one. The world of Generation X is simply too complex. The phenomenon was identified by Douglas Coupland in *Generation X* as "Option paralysis: The tendency, when given unlimited choices, to make none."

> For . . . [Brendan Gillan, a junior at the University of Michigan] nothing is simple anymore. Even ordering pizza means more than agonizing over toppings. The owner of Domino's Pizza, popular with many college students, is a staunch supporter of anti-abortion groups, a fact many students consider when they pick up their phones to order, Gillen says. Even simple consumerism has become complex, he says. The more you know and the more realizations you have, the harder life gets. You have to question everything. It creates an air of despair.[1]

Figure 8—10
All Products that Pollute the Environment
Should be Banned (% College Grads who agree)

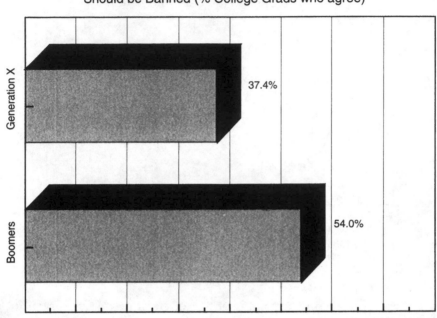

Source: Simmons Market Research Bureau:
1993 Study of Media and Markets

As a more diverse generation, Xers also have different political priorities. Blacks or immigrants may value improved employment opportunities more than they value the ideals of environmentalism. When students at Indiana University and the Student Environmental Action Coalition declared a proposed hazardous waste incinerator in Mississippi an act of "environmental racism" because of its location in a low-income area, their protests were resisted by black residents who wanted the jobs and the economic boost that the project would create.

In contrast to Boomers, who value "doing good," Generation X may be more comfortable with the goal to "do no harm." In other words, even when we do not know how to cure the environment, we can at least try not to make it any worse. By undertaking small, personal solutions (recycling paper, driving smaller cars) Xers can avoid making environmental pollution worse, without necessarily committing to fix the damage done by earlier generations.

In 1993, Converse All Stars designed a series of commercials for its popular shoes. The idea was a unique campaign targeted to twentysomethings, and executions featured groups of young people in big-city venues, most engaged in realistic, irreverent behavior. In one spot, a character wearing Converse All Stars spray-painted his name on the side of a building. The spots tested well with the proposed target audience, but Converse found in the research a strong, negative reaction to the spray-painting episode. The Generation X audience did not want to see one of their own deface a building.

The reaction to that small episode was, in fact, so negative that Converse edited it out of the commercial, although they kept the realistic city backdrop of graffiti-laden walls. Spray painting is an act that defaces the city environment. We may have to live with it, but we don't have to contribute to it. By reading their audience carefully, Converse discovered a truer way to reflect the underlying value system and avoided a marketing error. Listening can tell us a lot about these consumers, and Generation X appreciates such small signals.

There is little doubt that the perception of environmental harm can cost a product heavily with Generation X. Among Xers, nearly six out of ten college graduates report owning a new car. But, having grown up with gasoline shortages, smog, ozone alerts, and legislative efforts to regulate the auto industry, Generation X now has a real aversion to large cars. Both SMRB and JD Power report a clear preference for fuel-efficient performance and smaller-sized vehicles. (See Figure 8–11.)

While this skew is partially attributable to the lower income of Generation X versus older population segments, the bias toward small cars is expected to hold even as Xers become more affluent. Today, Generation X is moving from small, basic transportation toward sportier small cars with more options or to small trucks.

Trucks are a popular choice for younger adults and college students, particularly smaller pickups and sport utility vehicles. While a small truck may use as much gasoline as a large car, Generation X seems to find them less politically incorrect. Trucks have not only escaped the "gas guzzler" association which taints large cars, but

Figure 8–11
Index to U.S. Adults

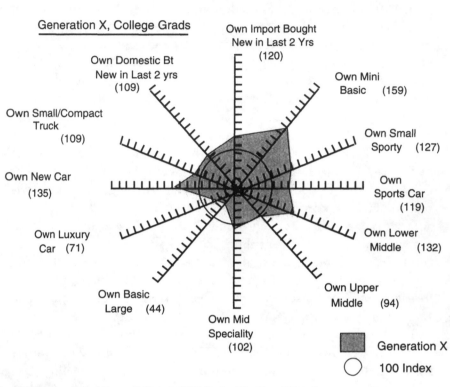

Source: Simmons Market Research Bureau: 1993 Study of Media and Markets

they also carry positive associations: the outdoors, useful pursuits, and a healthy lifestyle. (See Figure 8–12.)

In 1992, McDonald's was targeted by environmental activists who called attention to the harmful effects of the Styrofoam cups and cartons in which the fast-food giant dispensed so many sandwiches and hot drinks.

Many young parents were sympathetic to the issue, and there were calls for boycott. But what really caught MacDonald's attention, according to Pat Isaac, Midwest Regional Director, was when they began to receive letters from schools.

Figure 8–12
Own Small/Compact Trucks

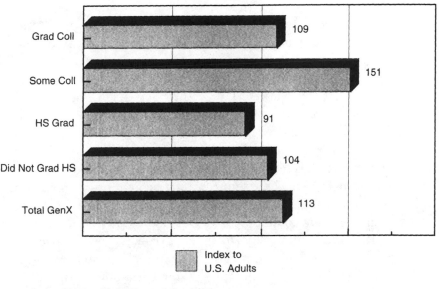

Grad Coll — 109

Some Coll — 151

HS Grad — 91

Did Not Grad HS — 104

Total GenX — 113

Index to U.S. Adults

Source: Simmons Market Research Bureau:
1993 Study of Media and Markets

"They were organized by young teachers," she said, "and whole classes were writing in to tell us they were not coming to MacDonald's anymore, unless we got rid of the styrofoam. Well, what will you do? This is a kid's business. That's what the business is all about."

McDonald's Corporation acted swiftly to reevaluate its packaging and quickly announced a change in policy. Today, it is likely that your Big Mac will come wrapped in cardboard or paper and your coffee in a heavy paper cup. The protest dissipated. And McDonald's is still a leader in the fast food business, partly because they understand the importance of listening to customers on an issue like this.

Marketers who seek the "big idea" must be careful in touting social programs to Generation X. If your product offers a real environmental advantage, it is probably good to point that out in your marketing effort. But nebulous hype will probably be perceived as just that. And programs that offer to donate funds or initiate movements to save the environment will likely have more appeal to Baby Boomers than to Generation X.

Environmental products with the greatest immediate potential may be those which offer help to Xers as they live and work in our deteriorated environment. Sunscreens, water filters, vitamins, and similar products can help Generation X cope with environmental dangers while we continue to search for more permanent solutions.

It is important for marketers to remember that Generation X comes out of a different history, with a different set of life experiences. Xers have therefore learned to cope using new skills and a different set of expectations. They are living their lives different ly than the way Boomers lived theirs at the same age, and the marketing implications which arise from that fact are important for us to note and to understand.

For example, Xers commonly spend an extended period of time as unmarried adults. Not only do they marry later, but in a sense, they become "adults" at a younger age, taking on greater responsibility while teenagers and enjoying greater autonomy both within the family and in society at large. While still in school, many are holding down jobs, contributing to the family finances, and sharing household chores. The majority of Xers become sexually active while still in their teens.[2]

In the Boomer generation, young and single was a brief and fleeting lifestage, often devoted to education or to military service. Xers are likely to remain single throughout their twenties and early thirties and to have very different experiences as single men and women. Military service is not compulsory in the 1990s, and during this decade of disarmament and drawing down, the armed services have become a less attractive career option. Nor does there currently exist any compelling national political issue to galvanize the youth of Generation X as Vietnam galvanized Boomers.

Instead, Xers finish their education and go to work as soon as they can. And, as working adults, they often enjoy a period of five to ten years during which some discretionary income is theirs alone to save or squander. With neither spouse nor children to support, with housing often provided by parents or shared with roommates, Generation X is relatively free to invest in travel, cars, clothing, entertainment, and in their own personal sense of style. Young single

Xers, especially those with college educations and steady jobs, represent a strong potential market for a wide range of goods and services—a better market, perhaps, than Boomers at the same age. Certainly, they place a great deal more emphasis on appearance and are, therefore, good potential markets for clothing, cosmetics, and personal grooming products. (See Figure 8–13.)

The context is entirely different for each generation. A thirty-year-old Boomer was likely to be furnishing a single family home for the needs of a growing young family, and making some personal sacrifice to do so. A thirty-year-old Xer may be debating whether to spend his cash on a vacation to Europe, updating his wardrobe, or buying a new motorcycle.

In clothing and apparel, Xers like simple, functional value. Women are more likely to buy cloth coats than fur—real or fake. They prefer sweat shirts and T-shirts to blouses and sweaters. Both sexes prefer plain old workout clothes to more upscale specialty garments like leotards or ski or tennis garb. For work, they buy less

Figure 8–13
Optimizing Personal Appearance

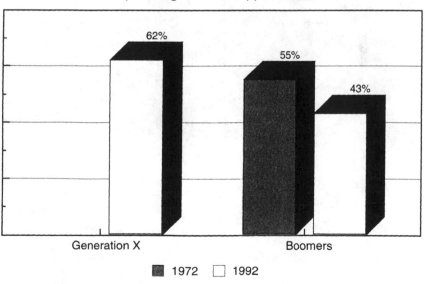

Generation X   Boomers

■ 1972   □ 1992

Source: Yankelovich Partners Inc, 1993

expensive two-piece suits off the rack, and the women are more likely to wear skirted suits than pants. Comfort takes precedence over glamour. (See Figure 8–14.)

Xers order from catalogs more than the average U.S. adult, but less often than the more affluent and busier Boomer. Despite the skew toward economical, functional clothes (understandable on lower incomes), Generation X does not seem to be excessively cautious about pennies. They are no more likely to use coupons than Boomers, except for tobacco, and use store brands slightly less often than Boomer grads do.

The bottom line is that Generation X is willing to pay for value

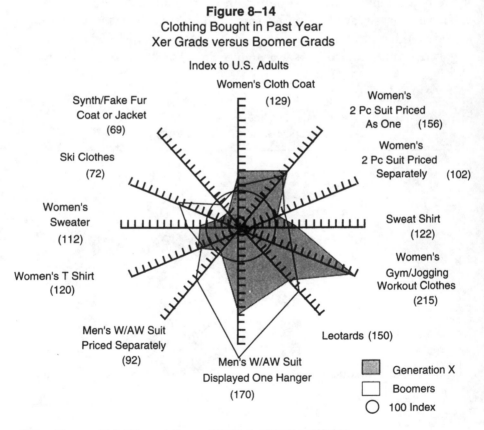

Figure 8–14
Clothing Bought in Past Year
Xer Grads versus Boomer Grads

Index to U.S. Adults

Women's Cloth Coat (129)

Synth/Fake Fur Coat or Jacket (69)

Women's 2 Pc Suit Priced As One (156)

Ski Clothes (72)

Women's 2 Pc Suit Priced Separately (102)

Women's Sweater (112)

Sweat Shirt (122)

Women's T Shirt (120)

Women's Gym/Jogging Workout Clothes (215)

Men's W/AW Suit Priced Separately (92)

Leotards (150)

Men's W/AW Suit Displayed One Hanger (170)

Generation X
Boomers
100 Index

Source: Simmons Market Research Bureau: 1993 Study of Media and Markets

or for brands that represent real value for the money. But as they express themselves through clothing, they often seem to be saying, "I'm too smart to fall for a designer label."

College grads in this group are exceptionally well traveled. SMRB reports that 64 percent of them took a domestic trip within the past year, and nearly one-third (29 percent) traveled abroad (including Hawaii and Alaska) within the past three years. No hippies with backpacks thumbing across the continent and crashing at youth hostels, Xers are as likely as mature Boomers to use travel agents, stay at hotels, or fly business class. Compared to Boomers, they are more likely to travel by rail, by boat, or by chartered plane. In fact, the only area of foreign travel where Xers do not *already* match Boomers is in business travel or accompanying one's spouse on a foreign business trip, and those categories are largely a matter of lifestage. (See Figure 8–15.)

The fondness of Generation X for travel, and their willingness to travel internationally with great regularity, is also an indication of the developing global marketplace and the international nature of the Generation X phenomenon. As they travel abroad, Xers find kindred souls in similar age groups wherever they go. And as the Internet crosses international borders with the ease of a telephone call, a Generation X–like phenomenon has been reported by Mc-Cann-Erickson offices in many developed countries: in England, throughout most of Western Europe, in the Scandinavian countries, and in Japan. The demographics are different. In the United Kingdom, for example, Generation X represents about half the adult population. Indeed, by 1998 Xer adults will exceed Boomer adults in virtually every developed country. While the generational personality may vary from country to country, a similar generation gap appears to exist in a wide variety of cultures.

In the United States, Generation X is much more concerned about their long-term economic prospects than Boomers were at the same age. Even in their twenties, many are planning for the future, anticipating an old age with no Social Security, soaring health costs, and shaky pensions. While investment options are limited for young and entry-level employees, Xers take the first opportunity to start individual retirement accounts, sometimes while still in college. In fact, saving for retirement is sometimes a higher priority

Figure 8–15
Foreign Travel
Xer College Grads vs. Boomer College Grads

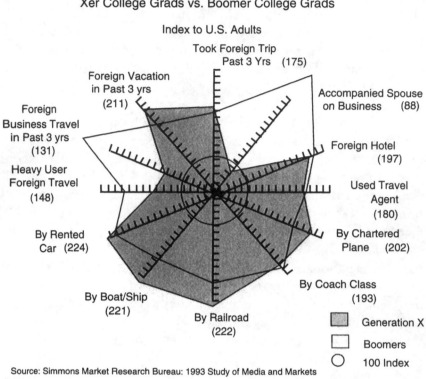

Index to U.S. Adults

Took Foreign Trip
Past 3 Yrs   (175)

Foreign Vacation
in Past 3 yrs
(211)

Accompanied Spouse
on Business   (88)

Foreign
Business Travel
in Past 3 yrs
(131)

Foreign Hotel
(197)

Heavy User
Foreign Travel
(148)

Used Travel
Agent
(180)

By Rented
Car (224)

By Chartered
Plane   (202)

By Boat/Ship
(221)

By Coach Class
(193)

By Railroad
(222)

Generation X

Boomers

100 Index

Source: Simmons Market Research Bureau: 1993 Study of Media and Markets

for them than other common banking services, like safe deposit boxes or savings certificates, i.e., CDs. (See Figure 8–16.)

> I'm not expecting any level of comfort to be handed to me. I have to make myself independent.
>
> —Rob McCarl, New York City

I talked to a reporter from *Business Week*, a young woman in her twenties. She told me she was worried about her IRA. She said all her friends were worried about their IRAs, and she asked me whether we used to worry about retirement and the Social Security system when we were young. I told her, no, we worried about whether Bob Dylan should have gone electric. They didn't even have IRAs when I was twenty.

Figure 8–16
Xers Who Personally Have

	Coll Grads		SomeColl		All Boomers	
	Percent	Index	Percent	Index	Percent	Index
Checking Acct/Bank	31.6	115	29.5	108	31.3	114
Savings Acct/Bank	28.3	113	24.8	99	26.8	107
401K Acct	10.4	152	7.3	106	9.5	139
Overdraft Protection	8.9	148	7.5	124	7.9	132
Safe Deposit Box	6.1	62	4.8	49	11.4	117
Savings Certif (CD)	5.5	51	6.3	57	10.3	94

Source: Simmons Market Research Bureau: 1993 Study of Media and Markets

But it is likely that Generation X will continue to feel this burden of economic uncertainty for the rest of their lives. Childhood disappointments have made their mark and stamped the generation with a general lack of confidence in the long-term ability of business, government, or so-called safety nets like Social Security or Medicare to provide for them in the future.

They were children when Jimmy Carter turned out the Christmas lights. The first gasoline shortages hit with full force just before they were old enough to get a driver's license. For many, there was the trauma and change of fortune associated with their parents' divorce. For others, school failed to live up to its billing. When they got to college, financial aid was scarce, and when they moved out into the job market, they couldn't find work. Since Generation X has been around, even the weather has been bad.

These experiences will remain a part of the Generation X psyche, just as the Great Depression was an indelible memory for children of the 1930s and marked their consumer behavior for the rest of their lives. So, too, these warnings, shortages, and disappointments will forever make Generation X cautious consumers, cost-conscious shoppers, and skeptical audiences for advertising.

9

Future X

Implications for Marketing

Xers are perhaps closer to their parents than any recent generation has been. Rather than breaking ties with parents during the turbulence of adolescence and moving on to new adult families, Xers tend to rebound after college and other brief experiences of independent living. Then, as adults, they must redefine their relationships with the same parents, siblings, stepparents, et al., they grew up with. That Xers tend to work out such relationships during the years they spend at home is demonstrated by the fact that nearly half of them continue to live at home through their late twenties.

In fact, Generation X is helping to form a new, extended American family, one which includes close friends, stepparents, adopted and half-siblings, live-in lovers, and a host of diverse relations. An important aspect of this new, extended family often involves a renewed bond between Generation X and older family members.

The *Details* Magazine Survey saw this strong connection in the responses of the Xers they surveyed: Half (51 percent) of Generation X said they "admire their parent(s) more than anyone else," and more than a quarter (29 percent) described their mother or father as "my best friend."

Clearly, even after Xers move out on their own, many continue to depend on an emotional and social connection with parents. The transition to adulthood is neither angry nor sudden, as evidenced by the large number of Xers who continue to receive financial help from Mom and Dad. (See Figure 9–1.)

151

Figure 9–1
What Kind of Financial Help
Do You Get from Your Parents?

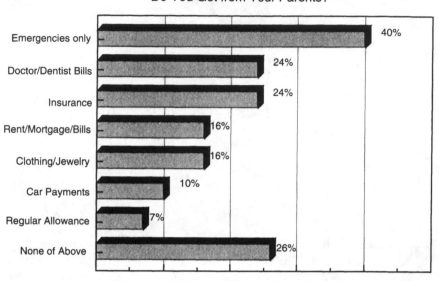

Source: Details Magazine National Survey 1993

Many Xers (45 percent of *Details* respondents) also feel an obligation to repay parents for the help they give, because this is an adult relationship, with benefits to both sides. Reciprocity can take many forms, but it often involves Generation X taking on continued responsibility for household chores, maintenance, and shopping. As their parents age, the need for such assistance does not diminish, but may in fact increase. And as Xers come of age, they may find their parents depend on them more, rather than less.

Because they remained at home longer, many marketers have underestimated the importance of Generation X as consumers. If marketers have not considered the degree to which the parent-child relationship changes over time, they may not have noticed that many Xers have become "designated decision makers" for their parents or other relatives. This may be especially true in those areas where young adults have particular expertise, i.e. electronic equipment, computers, or in some cases, automobiles. Since so many Xers were children of working parents, they were given early shopping chores. An Xer may begin by picking up some milk at the store, progress to specifying a new computer, and end by hiring a contractor to remodel the house for her parents or advising on the purchase of a new car.

Whether and when a child assumes some decision-making responsibility for a parent will also depend on the parent's situation and inclination. Boomers are often independent by nature, and the large number of working women means they are relatively more accomplished in business and money management than their own parents were. But Boomers are also stretched to maximum at the apex of their careers, with aging parents to care for and adult children at home. It is natural that they should turn sometimes to those children for assistance. So Xers are situated, physically and emotionally, to help handle their parents' assets, as well as their own, over a relatively long period of time.

And often, adult children of divorced parents have a lot of family to choose among. If an Xer cannot get along with his mother, he can join his father's family and adopt a stepmother. If he feels closer to his mother, he may remain attached to her relatives as well, including a new spouse, housemate, or significant other, and *his* relatives. Many Xers maintain contact with a large network of relatives and friends, including several different family branches. In this manner, a single Xer with a high degree of expertise about computers, for example, may consult in several households and be a significant influence on purchasing decisions in all of them.

When Generation X eventually marries, it will be later in life than Boomers did, and their marriages may represent a return to a more stable lifestyle than we have seen in recent decades. First of all, Xers are playing the statistics in favor of lasting marriages: They are marrying at a later age and hopefully increasing the maturity/stability of each partner. (See Figure 9–2.)

By delaying marriage until education is complete and careers have been established, they are increasing the economic stability of the future marriage. They are delaying the birth of their first child, which also helps to maximize resources. Both partners expect to work and to share in household chores, and that will make for less stressful partnerships.

As a result, young married couples should enjoy greater financial security, more discretionary income, less conflict, and more stable

Figure 9–2
Median Age at First Marriage

	Men	Women
1960	23	20
1970	23	21
1980	25	22
1991	26	24

Source: Statistical Abstract of the U.S. 1993

marriages than Boomers. Generation X may, indeed, achieve its goal of marriage for life. (See Figure 9–3.)

Marriage for Generation X will probably not mean the forma-

Figure 9–3
Attitudes Toward Marriage

	Percent Who Agree
When I get married, I expect to be married for life	89
To me, the twenties are the best time to marry and start a family	46
I'd like to get married as soon as possible	19
I see my twenties as the time to settle down and get my career going	60

Source: Details Magazine National Survey

tion of another totally separate nuclear family. Boomers who married earlier often saw getting married as another aspect of adolescent separation. Marriage was a badge of independence and adulthood, and many Boomers were therefore anxious to put space between their old family and their new spouse. Generation X will be more settled and more accustomed to the extended family that evolved during their bachelor years.

As they move into middle age, Generation X is likely to remain involved with their parents, even when established in separate households. While Boomers today find themselves sandwiched, torn between the needs of their adolescent children and the needs of their aging parents, Xers will find themselves in a slightly more positive situation, because they will have formed a broader network of resources. They will also find their Boomer parents less helpless, having come from a broader variety of work experience for men and women alike. Having renewed and redefined the older pattern of extended family, but in a more modern context, Generation X may be better equipped in the long run to handle life's more difficult stages.

In the workplace, Generation X will continue the balancing act between career and home but will keep in mind the lesson of their parents' example. Generation X does not question the achievements of Boomer women in the workplace, but they often question the price of those achievements. Boomer women, some of whom have spent a lifetime opening new opportunities for women, are understandably puzzled when Generation X women preface a statement with, "I'm not a feminist, but. . . ." Boomers are concerned when Generation X women are quick to claim the benefits of feminism and equally as quick to disavow any association with it.

Chris Meyers, head of Laine Meyers Associates, an advertising representative firm, notes that many young career women are focused on advancement but seem unwilling to go the distance, the way Boomer women did to achieve the next promotion or the bonus or the raise in pay.

"They have three years in the business, and they want their own talk show," says Chris. "They want your job. They want my job, but they don't want to pay the kind of dues we paid. They haven't got a clue what it was like—what we had to go through to get these jobs!"

Boomer men and women who have worked hard to gain the success they enjoy do not understand when an Xer expresses a reluctance to make personal sacrifices for the sake of career. What we face here is a version of the "grass is always greener" syndrome. Boomer women were willing to sacrifice some of the family life, which they had in oppressing abundance, in return for a chance at a career. Generation X women have a clear shot at the executive suite but often have been working since high school and long for a change of pace. They place a greater importance on the home and family life they missed as children and are unwilling to compromise that ideal for a job. While Xer women will continue to work, they will not sacrifice their personal lives or families to the degree that Boomer women did.

Marketers would be wise to note this temperature change, but should not read it as a return to the 1950s. Boomer women made the market for power suits, Rolex watches, Saabs, and BMWs. For Generation X, balance and perspective will be a primary goal. Look for continued emphasis on leisure activities, including family entertainment, economical and functional clothing, quality day care, and home offices.

Apartment furnishings and appliances in smaller or more portable configurations will be useful to young singles and young married couples alike. Small, economical automobiles like Geo Metro and the Chrysler Neon are already popular with this market.

Any product or service that feeds the need of young, single Xers to stay in touch and in control at the same time will do well: carphones, beepers and pagers, answering machines, computer mail, fax machines, and so forth are necessities—not luxuries—to Generation X.

Banks, insurance companies, and credit cards would do well to overcome their long-standing mistrust of applicants without credit ratings and to look for ways to provide services to Generation X. Their good work history, high aspirations, and consumer savvy will make them likely prospects and ultimately good customers.

Throughout the life cycle of Generation X, diversity will be an increasingly important factor. Products which recognize that individuals have different or special needs will continue to do well. The growth in the market for beauty products designed to meet the needs of black or Hispanic women is a good example. Ethnic foods are another, both in packaged foods and in ethnic restaurants. So, too, are music videos, language instruction materials, legal services, job placement agencies, and catalogs that cater to odd sizes.

From the standpoint of numbers, the emerging Hispanic market will be of paramount importance to marketers over the next decade. Those who offer mainstream products would do well to recognize that this $200 billion marketplace is on its way to becoming the largest ethnic minority in the United States, while the geographical concentration of Hispanics in large metropolitan areas makes them the majority of shoppers in some retail districts today.

Another large group just beginning to emerge is one that has never been targeted by mainstream marketers as a viable consumer group: the gay market. While homosexual men and women have remained a relatively invisible market segment to Boomers and older generations, the AIDS epidemic has acted as a galvanizing force during the 1980s—gay men and women have felt the need to come forward in defense of their special health care needs and to combat prejudice and misunderstanding about the gay community. Activism on behalf of gay civil rights has gained some support from both homosexual and heterosexual communities, and gay individuals are increasingly more willing to be publicly identified.

Most of these changes have taken place during the lifetime of Generation X. Indeed, the broad acceptance of sexual expression in the college-educated segment of twentysomethings is still largely unrecognized in the balance of American society. Bill Clinton stumbled upon this particular generational schism in the early days of his administration when he attempted to change the status of gays in the military.

According to Sarah Schulman, novelist, playwright, and gay activist, "If you come out in college there is an openly gay faculty member you can talk to and a gay student group, and you can even take Queer Studies 101. But in most states you still may not have your basic civil rights."[1]

Few reliable statistics exist on sexual orientation, but it is generally acknowledged that gays represent a potentially large market of upscale, well-educated professionals, perhaps as many as 12 million adults. Almost 40 percent of unmarried partners of homosexuals hold a college degree, compared with 18 percent of unmarried heterosexual partners and 13 percent of married spouses. While only

14 percent of the partners of gay men and 19 percent of the partners of gay women have less than a high school education, 21 percent of heterosexual spouses and 26 percent of heterosexual unmarried partners do not have a high school diploma.

Gay male couples have higher incomes than any other group, including married couples, traditionally the nation's most affluent family type.[2] The fact that Time-Warner, publishers of *Time*, *Life*, *Sports Illustrated*, and *People*, seriously considered the publication of a gay-oriented magazine is one measure of the serious marketing potential that is thought to exist. While Time-Warner judged in 1994 that the timing was not optimal for this publication, it is likely that another major publisher will undertake such an enterprise in the near future.

According to Tony Kushner, Tony award–winning author of Broadway's *Angels in America*, "I get the sense that these kids have crossed over the river. There is a new generation arriving whose visceral ideas of homosexuality will be completely different."[2]

Whether or not your company chooses to target gays as potential customers, it will become increasingly important to avoid negative stereotypes and unwitting offensiveness. For Generation X, this market is simply another factor to deal with in an increasingly complicated world.[3]

Commercials have been a part of their world since they were young children, and to Xers, advertising is another of those familiar markers that orient them and give them something to talk about. Of course, advertising can be stupid, misleading, offensive, or, worst of all, boring. Advertising can also be clever, amusing, or entertaining, and occasionally an ad actually tells you something you wanted to know.

But there is, among Generation X, a sense of information overload, and to some degree the rejection of hype, of advertising, is a self-protective mechanism.

> After being on the phone all day, you go home and get three calls from these direct marketers. Then you go out to the mailbox and 42 solicitations fall out—you can't get away from it. You can't even take a walk without somebody shoving a leaflet in your hand. I really worry that

this kind of overstimulation will have an effect, that it leads to some kind of sensory death or something.
—Chris Chalk, Chicago

It is the intrusive nature of 1990s advertising that Generation X objects to. They expect to see ads on television and in magazines, but they are a generation which likes to feel in control. They cherish their answering machines, VCRs, CDs, and remote-control devices because these things allow *them* to decide what to focus on. If they want to watch your commercial, they will. But don't try to force-feed them, because they won't stand for it. Somehow, they will find the technology to sidestep your intrusion. In the words of Douglas Rushkoff:

> It is a conscious effort to avoid engaging in anything that requires descent into the rat race or consumerist angst, a neo-Buddhism where attachments of any kind break the awareness so valuable to surfers of a consumer culture. It is an ability to derive meaning from the random juxtaposition of TV commercials, candy wrappers, childhood memories, and breakfast treats. . . .[4]

Generation X doesn't dislike advertising. They dislike *hype*. They dislike overstatement, self-importance, hypocrisy, and the assumption that *anyone* would want to be disturbed at home by a salesman on the telephone. To the degree that contemporary advertising is guilty of hype, advertising will have to change.

If you wish Generation X to adopt your product, it must be perceived as a useful product—not one to be purchased for reasons of status or to make a statement, but one to be purchased to fulfill a genuine need. Never mind that young people and others tend to get their wants and their needs mixed up—it is perception we are talking about here.

Just as Generation X is antihype and skeptical of social movements, so do they reject the concept of conspicuous consumption. "Keeping up with the Joneses" has never been a goal for them. They are too busy keeping up with their own parents.

Besides, in 1994, the Joneses are far more likely to be the Wongs, the Abdullahs, or the Garcias, to speak another language, and to have far different aspirations, anyway. Products that hype their own success with copy points like "the best-selling mousetrap in America" or "the mousetrap for upscale vermin" are not likely to cut any ice with Generation X.

It has been observed that Generation X has no heroes. Unlike Boomers, Xers do not tend to idolize their role models. With unrelenting pragmatism they see the whole person, warts and all. *Details* found that not a single Xer—not one—wished to change places with Madonna or Michael Jackson. (See Figure 9–4.)

Not only have Xer icons been relatively short-lived phenomena, but those who do last seem destined to a life of continuing media abuse: Sinead O'Connor, Andre Agassi, Roseanne Arnold, Shannon Doherty, Dennis Rodman, and so forth. This may make it difficult to employ a celebrity spokesperson in advertising directed to this audience.

Generation X likes to keep their distance, and if they value star power, they also value detachment. While they follow the rich, the famous, and the infamous alike, they do not identify with them and would certainly have no illusions about changing places with them. In fact, Generation X actively pursues the deflation of the ideal. No icon and certainly no commercial is safe from their irony, their sar-

Figure 9–4
Opinions/Goals

If you were given one wish from the list below, which one would you choose?	Percent
Live happily ever after	32
Inherit $10 million	27
Find a cure for cancer	20
Find a cure for AIDS	19
Trade places with President Clinton	2
Trade places with Madonna or Michael Jackson	0

Source: Details Magazine National Survey

casm, or their remote control. These are the tools with which Generation X keeps the world in perspective.

On the other hand, Xers have a decided preference for the elevation of the ordinary. They like to see the common man come out on top. And they particularly love to see one of their own get ahead. Witness their continued respect for such low-key role models as Bill Gates, of Microsoft, or Matt Groening, creator of the Simpsons. Such success at an early age gives them hope for their own situation. Many Xers were also charmed by the common-man-with-common-sense appeal of Ross Perot in 1992, and 21 percent of Xers cast their vote for Perot, as compared to 18 percent of Boomers.

Regardless of the segment(s) targeted by the marketers of any individual product, the diversity of this generation will remain a formidable challenge. Rather than defining targets in terms of primary, secondary, and tertiary levels, in the future targets will probably be defined as conglomerates of equally important, but diverse segments. Each segment will be desirable for reasons that may not be shared by other segments of the market. Marketers may need to vary product design, distribution, cost, and promotion depending on the part of the prospect group they wish to conquest or to preserve.

As U.S. Budget Director Richard Reich is fond of saying, "There are two kinds of people: those who don't know the future, and those who don't know they don't know the future." The jury is still out on the ultimate economic success or failure of Generation X, and that is beyond our control. In the meantime, we have put a lot of energy for a lot of years into scaring our kids about how poor they can expect to be when they grow up. No wonder the polls show a lack of consumer optimism! Perhaps we need to take a new tack. Perhaps we should stop telling everybody under the age of thirty-five that they have to settle for less, and concentrate instead on helping them discover what business and industry can do for them as consumers and as a generation of responsible adults.

10

The Future of Advertising

I have become fascinated lately with a speech pattern linguists call "the rising inflection." For those who may be unfamiliar with this term, it describes the habit of allowing one's voice to rise at the end of a sentence. It makes an ordinary declarative sentence sound like a question. Thus, "we received your proposal?" has the identical inflection as "Can we go to Disneyland?"

There is a slight pause at the end of the sentence—a pause not long enough to allow more than acknowledgement from the listener but slightly longer than one would normally leave between declarative sentences. I have observed that this is a common speech pattern among Generation X, especially among white men and women.

On the Coasts and among more highly educated Xers, the pattern often incorporates an exaggerated pronunciation of consonants, so the "s" is more sibilant and "th" more breathy. The overall effect is that the speaker is being very careful to phrase her thoughts. And of course, the speech is peppered with qualifying phrases: perhaps, like, sort of, just, you know, totally. Sometimes these modifiers are strung together in a phrase with the rising inflection, to create a sentence such as, "He's just, sort of, like, you know, clueless?"

Xers speak this way because they find it gentler and more accommodating. The rising inflection, the slight pause, and the modifiers are intended to acknowledge that the listener might have a different opinion, an opposing point of view. Xers, more sensitive to di-

163

verse points of view, make a conscious effort not to co-opt the listener, not to assume that he or she holds the same opinion. This hesitant tone is meant to prompt a response from the listener—feedback. It means something like, "you may not agree with this part, but hear me out, ok?"

Unfortunately, that is not the way most Boomers hear it. To Boomer ears, this speech pattern sounds uncertain, hesitant, questioning. It is as if the speaker wasn't sure of what he was saying. To Boomer ears, this is a speaker begging for advice, for direction. This is a speaker who wants to be told what to do. But Xers know perfectly well what they think, and Boomers who rush in with unsolicited advice are likely to encounter resistance and/or resentment from an Xer, who was only trying to be polite. This is a common example of how the generations misunderstand each other in very basic ways.

Just as Xers make subtle changes to the way we speak—by changing the intonation, the cadence of our language—so the contribution of young marketing professionals to the broader world of communications will be subtle. Nevertheless, we will find our world changed. If Boomers, as a group, tested every institution they encountered, dismantling in the process much of the foundation of 1950s society, the task for Generation X will be the renovation of these institutions. So, too, it is this next generation of media and marketing executives who must decide what to save and what to discard from today's disorganized heritage of conventional marketing techniques, radical think, and pop psychology.

When Generation X inherits the advertising business, I hope they will change its image. As advertising and marketing move toward becoming an interactive exchange of information, it will become more user friendly, less artificial, and less intrusive. As the technology changes, Generation X will have an opportunity to impact both the process and the face of the business. Perhaps advertising will return to its original purpose, information, and eventually shed the reputation for manipulation, annoyance, and questionable veracity. Perhaps not.

One thing is clear: the more advertising clings to the "newest, biggest, baddest" model that dominates today, the less successful we will be in convincing Generation X that advertising is an honest and reliable source of information. And the longer we patronize

Generation X with stereotyped portrayals that ignore their economic clout and marketing savvy, the higher the price we will pay in long-term market share.

Boomers like to make commercials that reference the idyllic past or envision some space-age, Yuppie utopia. Many like to reminisce about the good old days, while others speculate about the future. This behavior is appropriate to the Boomer life-phase. But Generation X lives solidly in the present. They even tend to speak in the present tense:

> I'm down at the mall, ok? And I see this guy walking out of the Denny's with Sharon? And, you're never going to believe this, but it turns out to be John, remember from the concert last week? And he goes, "I like your hair". And I'm like, "Right!" I got this incredibly stupid perm, and I look like some blonde Fizzie-Pop, you know?
> —Conversation overheard in a restaurant

If advertisers would successfully communicate with these new markets, they will need help from the people who live there. But it remains to be seen whether Xers will be around when Boomer marketers need them the most. It is clear already that Generation X does not have an unqualified love for the disciplines of marketing and advertising. Indeed, advertising in particular has such strong negative connotations for Generation X that it will become increasingly difficult to attract and to keep good marketing, creative, and media talent from this younger generation. Those who do stay claim increasingly that they do it for the money rather than for the work itself. Most view a career in advertising as a transitional phase, a path to more meaningful employment opportunities.

It is in this area that Boomers can offer the most meaningful assistance to the Xers in their own companies. In their midlife quest for power and affluence, in the midst of fallout from acquisitions, mergers, stunning client defections, and mind-numbing technological development, many Boomers have allowed themselves to become cynical and jaded about the business they practice. In their push for greater cost control, education of the next generation has fallen far behind as a priority. Training programs, tuition reimbursement, mentoring, have been replaced by "human resources" raiding parties whose specialty is to find semideveloped talent in other companies and open the bidding. Generation X has seldom been exposed in any meaningful way to the purpose of marketing. They are largely ignorant of any connection between advertising and economic development.

I spoke at a Generation X Marketing Conference in New York in 1994. The conference itself was later critiqued by a young writer, Nathaniel Wice, in *The GenX Reader*. Mr Wice cleverly termed my presentation "bathetic." "For [Ritchie], 'invisibility' refers not to the lack of government services for young people, but a paucity of twentysomething ad campaigns."

I obviously had failed to make clear the connection between marketing products to Generation X and creating jobs for them. I trust that, since our young writer has now found work as a critic of Generation X marketing conferences and as a publisher of his own *GenX* magazine, he now sees that connection in a very personal way. It is essential to the future of our business that other Generation X marketers also realize that connection.

Generation X correctly perceives marketing and advertising as powerful forces in contemporary society. What we Boomers need to make clear is that these forces can be used in the service of positive change as well as for less noble goals. Here Boomers need to shake off their prejudices about "the younger generation," to remind themselves why marketing or advertising was a good career choice, and to open a dialogue with their younger associates about the beneficial and ethical practice of advertising and marketing. Agencies and clients alike might reevaluate the long-term economic benefits of investments in training, mentoring, and employee education. To Generation X, these benefits are among the most attractive in selecting which agency to join, or which company to stay with, even when the head-hunters call.

Most Xers will acknowledge the contributions of advertising in the war against drug abuse. From the clumsy "Just say no!" campaign to the much more successful "This is your brain on drugs," public service advertising has encouraged many Xers to grow up clean and sober. Most Xers will admit that advertising, perhaps more than any other single strategy, has affected their opinions and their behavior in regard to smoking cigarettes or driving when drunk. Most recognize the ability of advertising to affect the outcome of elections—the benefit here may depend upon your point of view. Nevertheless, a discipline that has the power to shape public opinion, even a little, should not be left to the discretion of a new generation of professionals to whom we have imparted little or no background in ethical practice or sound business theory.

In the business of marketing, Generation X now thoroughly owns the low-level, entry-level, clerical, and trainee end of the job spectrum. A few leading-edge Xers have begun to break through to mid-level positions of responsibility. Many were hired at depressingly low wages during the recession-shocked late 1980s or early 1990s, and most have seen their careers stalled for the past three or four years. Agencies and other companies who take action now to motivate, train, inspire, and reward their younger employees, will be building loyalty among the next generation of marketing executives. Those who continue to ignore that potential work force may find that in the long run they have no qualified candidates to replace aging Boomer executives.

But Xers have important contributions to make long before they reach the executive suite. Now that Generation X has sparked an interest from major marketers, and with continuing economic growth, prospects should begin to brighten for most twentysomethings. As marketers and the media turn their attention to this vast new market, the need for a younger perspective, for personal expertise on the generational experience, will no doubt take on a greater urgency. And who better to comment on the experience of Generation X than Xers themselves?

If Xers can gather the skills necessary to communicate with their Boomer associates, and if Boomers can learn to listen more effectively, each generation stands to benefit enormously. In the workplace, Generation X will continue to insist upon balance. The days when an advertising agency might expect its younger employees to burn themselves out over endless nights and weekends to produce a new campaign or a new media plan are long gone. Too much emphasis on crisis management will more often cause Generation X to seek another line of work—one that allows some personal freedom and some time to grow.

I recognize this as an essentially healthy trend. I believe that sufficient leisure helps an employee to remain productive and creative. At the same time, too much emphasis upon personal freedom may fail to instill the work ethic necessary to the survival of service-based companies, like advertising agencies. Responsibility toward one's clients or customers, and the responsibility of the marketing professional for the customer's health, safety, and well-being are values that can only be inculcated by example and by the clear articulation of these goals as a vision of the company.

If Generation X is skeptical, they are also clear-sighted and smart. If they are less idealistic, they are also great practical strategists and good negotiators. If they play hard, they also work hard. On balance, they will infuse our business with a broader range of opinions, a more diverse workforce, greater technological expertise, and a more accommodating language. The future is in their hands.

I have few qualms about leaving the business to the next generation, now that I can see their faces. If Jerry Atkin could see me now, he would be surprised at how far that single "State of the Agency" presentation has evolved. I began this project with some trepidation, an uneasiness about these purple-haired people, and a great deal of embarrassment about my own ignorance. I have come away encouraged, enlightened, and optimistic about the future.

References

Chapter Two

1. William Strauss and Neil Howe, *Generations: The History of America's Future, 1584–2069*, William Morrow and Company, Inc., 1991.
2. Harm du Blij, *Good Morning America*, ABC News, January 27, 1993.
3. Landon Y. Jones "Great Expectations and the Baby Boom Generation" Coward, McCann and Geoghegan, 1980.
4. Watts Wacker, Yankelovich Partners, Inc.
5. Neil Howe and Bill Strauss, *13th Gen: Abort, Retry, Ignore, Fail?* Vintage Books, 1993.
6. Douglas Coupland, *Generation X: tales for an accelerated culture* St. Martin's Press, 1991.

Chapter Three

1. Simmons Market Research Bureau: 1993 Study of Media and Markets.
2. *Cosmopolitan Report "The Changing Lives of American Women,"* Hearst Corporation, 1986.
3. Statistical Abstract of the United States 1991.
4. Neil Howe and Bill Strauss, *13th gen: abort, retry, ignore, fail?* Vintage Books, 1993.
5. Jeff Giles, "Generalizations X," *Newsweek*, June 6, 1994.
6. Bradford Fay, Research Director, "Generation X: What's New, What's Not," Roper Starch Worldwide, May 25, 1993.
7. Details Magazine National Survey, 1993.

Chapter Four

1. Hanna Liebman, "Forget the X, Please," *Media Week*, August 2, 1993.
2. Michele Galen et al., "White, Male, and Worried," *Business Week*, January 31, 1994.

3. Ibid.
4. Hugh Gallagher, "Seven Days and Seven Nights Alone with MTV" *The GenX Reader* (Douglas Rushkoff ed.) Ballantine Books, 1994.
5. Julianne Malveaux, "Boomer Times: Different Strokes," *Emerge*, March 1993, p. 19.
6. Ibid.
7. Stephen Holden, "A Gay Cultural Festival Banishes the Silence," *The New York Times*, June 17, 1994.

Chapter Five

1. Ed Weiner et al., *The TV Guide TV Book: 40 Years of the All-Time Greatest Television Facts, Fads, Hits, and History*, Harper Perennial, 1992.
2. Raymond Mungo, *Famous Long Ago: My Life and Hard Times with Liberation News Service*, Beacon Press, 1970.
3. Gerald Howard, editor, *The Sixties: Art, Politics, and Media of Our Most Explosive Decade*, Paragon House, 1991.
4. Harry Castleman and Walter J. Podrazik, *Harry and Wally's Favorite TV Shows*, Prentice-Hall Press, 1989.
5. Gerald Howard, editor, *The Sixties: Art, Politics, and Media of Our Most Explosive Decade*, Paragon House, 1991.

Chapter Six

1. *Les Brown's Encyclopedia of Television*, 3rd ed., Visible Ink Press, 1992.
2. Ibid.
3. Ibid.
4. The Times Mirror Center for People and the Press, "TV Violence: More Objectionable In Entertainment Than In Newscasts" March 23, 1993.
5. Julian Dibbell, "Classic Rock," *Details*, July 1991.
6. Castleman and Podrazik. p. 20.
7. Jefferson Morley, *"Twentysomething,"* *Washington City Paper*, February 19–25, 1988.
8. Camille Paglia, "Riot Grrrls", Strauss and Howe 13th gen, p. 156.

Chapter Seven

1. Douglas Rushkoff, *The GenX Reader*, Ballantine Books, 1994.

Chapter Eight

1. Elizabeth Lee, "Generation X," *U, The National College Magazine*, May 1993.

Chapter Nine

1. Stephen Holden, "A Gay Cultural Festival Banishes the Silence," *The New York Times*, June 17, 1994.
2. Ibid.
3. Margaret Usdansky, "Gay Couples, by the numbers," *USA Today*, April 12, 1993.
4. Douglas Rushkoff. p. 6.

Index

Action for Children's Television, 87, 96
Advertising business, 165–167
All in the Family, 3, 24, 70, 92, 102
American Bandstand, 69
Apparel, 146, Fig 8–14
Atkin, Jerry, 2
Automotive, 142–143, Figs 8–11, 8–12

Baby Boom
   alternative media, 68
   birth years, 16
   causes, 81
   education, 32, Fig 3–3
   homogeneity, 30
   network television, 63, 80, Fig 5-4
   new technology, 121
   percent of adult population, 22, 27, Fig 2–3
   percent of target audience, 27–28, Fig 3–1
   population, 16–17, Fig 2–1
   product usage, 78
Beavis and Butthead, 117
Beverly Hills 90210, 80, 109, Fig 6–6
Birth cohort, 15, 21

Birth control, 36
Black Enterprise, 75, 77
Brady Bunch, The, 102
Brand loyalty, 130–131, Fig 8-1, 8-2
Buttafucco, Joey, 108

Cable television, 81, 115, Fig 7–1
Channel surfing, 117, 127
Children's television, 64–65, 86, 94–98
Cosby Show, The, 72, 80, Fig 5–4
Coupland, Douglas, 6, 25
Courtship of Eddie's Father, The, 74

Day care, 37
Divorce, 40, Fig 3–8

Ed Wynn Show, The, 92
Environmentalism, 136–140, 142, Figs 8–7, 8–8, 8–9, 8–10, 8–11
Extended family, 153

Father Knows Best, 69
Fertility, 31, Fig 3–2

Financial services, 148–149,
     Fig 8–16

Gay market, 157–158
Gekko, Gordon, 78, 103
General Hospital, 98
Generation X
   (in the) advertising business,
      165–167
   attitudes toward media, 113,
      122, 159
   attitudes toward parents, 151
   birth rates, 37, Fig 3–6
   birth years, 16, 37, Fig 3–6
   childhood, 36–46, 86
   conformity, 132–134, Figs 8–3,
      8–4, 8–5
   designated decision makers,
      152
   earnings potential, 23, 44, 47,
      Fig 3–12
   education 42, Fig 3–9
   environmentalism, 136–140,
      142, Figs 8–7, 8–8, 8–9,
      8–10, 8–11
   heros, 160
   households, non–traditional,
      43, 44, 48, 59, 74, 153,
      Fig 3–11
   income, 47, 55, 57, Fig 3–12
   label, 9
   marriage, 43–45, 59, 144, 154,
      Figs 3–12, 9–2, 9–3
   network television, 63
   new technology, 121
   parental support, 152, Fig 9–1
   percent of adult population, 22,
      27, Fig 2–3
   percent of population, 19,
      Figs 2–1, 2–2, 2–7
   percent of target audience,
      27–28, Fig 3–1
   population, 16–17
   poverty, 41
   product usage, 27, 45, 130–133,
      142, Fig 8–1, 8–2, 8–3, 8–4
   risk-taking, 135, Fig 8–6
   single adults, 151
   speech patterns, 163
   work ethic, 41, 46, 59, 155
GI Bill, 32

Happy Days, 74
Hispanic Business, 75
Howdy Doody, 65
Howe, Neil and Strauss, William,
   16

I Spy, 72

Jeffersons, The, 70, 72
Julia, 72

King, Rodney, 109

Laverne and Shirley, 74
Leave it to Beaver, 30, 69

Madonna, 104, 160
Magazines circulation, 83,
   Fig 5–6
Mass media, 63, 66, Fig 5–1
Maude, 70, 92, 97
Media hype, 114
Mickey Mouse Club, 69
Minorities in the media, 6, 72,
   76–77
Mod Squad, 72

Monday Night Football, 91
Ms Magazine, 24, 76
My Three Sons, 69

Network television, 82, Fig 5–5
   Nielsen ratings, 90, 109,
      Fig 6–6
   programming, 90–94, 99,
      100–101, Fig 6–3, 6–4
   quiz shows, 88–89
   scatter, 89–90
Northern Exposure, 109,
   Fig 6–6
NYPD Blue, 99

Odd Couple, The, 74
One Day at a Time, 74, 97

Peer personality, 15, 17–18, 39
Personal products, 145, Fig 8–3
Population of
   Baby Boom, 16–17, 22, 27–28,
      Fig 2–1, 2–3, 3–1
   Generation X, 16–17, 19, 22,
      27–28, Figs 2–1, 2–2, 2–3,
      3–1

Radio, 69, Fig 5–2
Ren and Stimpy, 117
Rolling Stone, 24, 67, 116

Saturday Night Live, 80
Seinfeld , 109, Fig 6–6
Seven Sisters, 66, Fig 5–1
Silent Generation, 11, 15
$64,000 Question, The, 88

Soap operas, 98
Strauss, William and Howe, Neil,
   16

Television
   color, 95, Fig 6–2
   interactive, 107, 126
   multi–set households, 87,
      Fig 6–1
   number of channels, 115,
      Fig 7–1
   tabloid tv, 80, 105–106, 122,
      Figs 5–4, 6–5
   violence, 93, 100–101,
      Figs 6–3, 6–4
Texaco Star Theatre, 92
Thirtysomething, 80
Three's Company, 74
Travel, 147–148, Fig 8–15

VCRs, 81, 118–120, Fig 7–2
Vietnam, 17–18, 35–36
Violence on television, 93,
      100–101, Figs 6–3, 6–4
Voicemail, 123

Women
   education, 35, Fig 3–5
   percent of new car buyers,
      78–79, Fig 5–3
   (in the) workforce, 33, 37–38,
      47, 54, Figs 3–4, 3–7, 3–13
Wonder Years, The, 3, 79
World War II, 32

Your Show of Shows, 92
Yuppies, 78

Acknowledgements

I would like to recognize the contribution of the many friends and business associates without whose assistance this book could not have been completed. It is with sincere gratitude that I acknowledge the following individuals and organizations:

Greg Michaels, who was the first to believe in Generation X.

My chief research assistant, Terry Chaney of McCann-Erickson, who sees more than most people do.

My good friends Sean Fitzpatrick and Bob Guccione, Jr, both busy writers who generously made time to encourage a novice.

All the people of McCann-Erickson for their generous support and continued encouragement.

The great media libraries and librarians at Lintas:Campbell-Ewald and *USA Today*.

My editor Beth Anderson and her assistant Jennifer Shulman for their wise and patient work.

The many fine media and research organizations who contributed background materials, including: McCann-Erickson, Worldwide, especially Ira Carlin, Worldwide Media Director; General Motors; *Details* Magazine, especially Mitchell Fox and Michael Perlis, Publishers; Simmons Market Research Bureau: 1993 Study of Media and Markets; *Manscan: Three Generations of Men*, a proprietary research study sponsored by *Men's Health Magazine* and conducted by DYG, Inc.; *The Cosmopolitan Report*, "The Changing Lives of American Women"; Yankelovich Partners, Inc.; The A.C. Nielsen Co.; Audit Bureau of Circulation; Roper Starch Worldwide, Inc.; Times-Mirror Center for The People and The Press; and the Radio Advertising Bureau.

Printed in the United States
By Bookmasters